JESUS.

[PERIOD]

Making Jesus the Center of Your Ministry

Beth Frank
and Others

Jesus. [Period]: Making Jesus the Center of Your Ministry

Published by KidzMatter
432 East Val Lane, Marion, IN 46952

Printed in the United States of America

978-1-0880-6156-5 (Paperback)

Jesus. [Period] Logo by 1230 Media
Cover design and interior layout by Nicole Jones - kneecoalgrace@gmail.com
Edited by Amber Pike - amberpike.org

[TABLE OF CONTENTS]

JESUS. [PERIOD]

THE WHY

Ryan and Beth Frank

[Jesus Christ is the same yesterday, today, and forever.
-Hebrews 13:8]

Ministry is demanding. (Life is demanding!) For most of us serving and volunteering in kidmin, we live life with the competing pressures of the church we work at, the pastor we serve, and possibly the denomination our church belongs to. In addition to all of this is the pressure of providing programming for the families of your church and community. We also balance the demands of our own family and personal life. In the midst of doing our best to serve and love others, we can get so caught up in the demands of the work that we begin to forget our why. It's always important, especially in the sometimes difficult and always demanding world of ministry, that we focus on our why.

Why?

Today it seems like there is a very pervasive church culture that most North American churches fit into. That culture makes it easy for all of us who attend to know pretty much what to expect. For example, on any given Sunday I know that I could walk into several different churches in my community and...

1. Be greeted at the door by greeters who are on the "hospitality team."
2. Have a small group time or class for my elementary age children in which they will bring home a "take home paper" and possibly a piece of candy.
3. Experience some type of music and worship.
4. An edgy guy, probably wearing plaid (ok, I'm sorry, we said it), will deliver a sermon on stage, possibly with a screen.
5. I will get a bulletin if the church is a little more traditional, scrolling video announcements if the church is more edgy, and both bulletin and scrolling announcements if the church is trying to appeal to both the traditional and edgy.
6. The offering plates will be passed.
7. I will be invited to be a part of some type of small group Bible study or meeting through the week.

This is all great, and we don't mean to strip away all the important work that ministry leaders do week after week and simplify it into a few bullet points. There is a lot that happens at church each week. A LOT! The programming and the logistics required to make sure that programming runs is intense. But imagine with us for a few minutes if we strip all that away. No church building, no denomination, no programming. What of our ministries would be left? Would people still be being effectively reached with the love of Jesus? Could we dynamically share the hope of scriptures?

Without a building and/or programming, would the families in your church still be actively doing life together with Jesus? Would life transformation still be happening?

My (Beth) grandfather was a pastor in our community for close to 40 years. He started in the 50's in a rural area at a small, country church. By the time he left, there were large buildings, a large outreach bus ministry, and a Christian school. He left because of a massive church split that is still painful for me to process many years later. This church now has a weekly attendance well below 20. The last time I walked through the Sunday school rooms they were covered in dust and there was a banner with a date five years in the past - desolate and sad. My grandpa is now in heaven. That church building sits about 30 miles from my house. I sometimes feel the urge to drive by and go down memory lane. My grandpa was a huge force in my life, and in a way, I feel closest to him there where he spent so much of his time and energy during his life. When I go past, I am reminded of so many things. But what strikes overwhelmingly is that ministry isn't about a building or a place. Sometimes in our North American church culture, we can get so focused on the church we are serving at and the programming that we are offering, that we forget the why. What is the why? It's about the people; the people knowing Jesus. [period]. Have the people experienced Jesus in a real and life changing way? Have the people in that church building, whether it be new and massive or a simple country church, bonded into a community? Is that community doing life together, loving and living for Jesus?

Now, well past 70 years from when my grandpa started as a college interim filling the pulpit on Sundays, there is still a legacy of people. I still know of churches across the country and globe whose pastors came to love Jesus because of meeting my grandpa in a service at that little country church. In my community, I meet people who will say to me, "I went to your Grandpa's church and that's where my life changed". I also meet people that never attended church with Grandpa, but they say, "your grandpa came and changed my tire, or visited me in the hospital."

I just heard someone this week say how he drove to a neighboring state to visit someone in the hospital who had never attended the church. A community of people still exists that love Jesus and serve him because of their time at a little country church.

Now, sadly, the church building is empty and the ministry is practically dead. In our human eyes that can really look like failure. Like, what was the point of this man coming and serving passionately in a small rural area for his lifetime only to have it end is such a tragic way? A once thriving church is now dead, years later, because of a painful church split. Money, time, and hard labor spent on large buildings that now sit empty and falling down may seem in man's economy as a waste. And if we were building a kingdom for a man, then yes, this would be a huge failure; some could even say a waste. Thankfully though, Jesus. [period]! It wasn't about the beautiful buildings. It wasn't about the complex programming. It was about Jesus and the people that met him there and were changed because of it.

I walked through the buildings again about a year ago, probably for the last time, and it's strangely healing and comforting. It's comforting because it's such a strong picture that we don't serve for the tangible. We don't pour our hearts out for programs that will inevitably lose their cutting edge. We serve because Jesus is at the core and heart of all that we do. At the end of the day, it's all about the message. The message should be preeminent. The point of the church building, the denomination, and all the programming is to assist us in the great commission. The church is so much bigger than a building, a denomination, or a program. Because without Jesus, it's just an empty church building; and without him, it's just belonging to a club that's called a church denomination. It's about the message and the radical transformation Jesus is doing in your life, church, and community.

Someday, the classroom you teach in week after week will empty for the last time. The church doors will close and what will be left? Jesus. [period]. And that's what will make all the difference for now and for eternity. If someone in the next generation walks through the dusty halls of your church, may those halls echo with stories of hope, healing, grace, and life-changing love. May all the uncovered artifacts whisper Jesus, Jesus, Jesus. [period]

Because without Jesus, it's just fun and games…

Ok, we are kidmin people and isn't it mandatory that we love fun and games? It's probably on some of your resumes that you can create curriculum that is fun and engaging! When you work with kids, and specifically kids in large groups, you need to be able to manufacture fun out of thin air sometimes. Fun during kid's church seems like a good goal, a necessary goal, even. But what is the goal of the game and the function of the fun? We have not succeeded if kids leave our Sunday morning experience only excited about the fun that they had. It must go beyond that. Kids should leave Sunday mornings excited and passionate about what they have heard, learned, and EXPERIENCED. How can we be sure though that we have gone beyond fun and games to the heart? Was the fun or the game an avenue to a child experiencing the presence of Jesus?

Through the years, I think that children's ministry in general gets a bad rap for being the fun and games department of the church, which to some extent should be true. Little people, by their very nature, are fun beings and are attracted like bees to honey when there is something fun and exciting going on in a room. A lot of us attend conferences and trainings about how to add more fun to our curriculum and how to bring the Bible to life through games. (This isn't a bad thing!) I have heard it said many times that it is a sin to bore kids with the Bible, and I absolutely agree. But without Jesus at the heart of our game time, it's just a game. A fun game, some years from now, might be remembered by the kids in your ministry with fondness and nostalgia, but it probably won't be remembered as life-changing. If it's just fun and it doesn't lead children to knowing Jesus and experiencing his presence, then what is the point?

Experiencing Jesus is the goal.

As kidmin leaders, we don't just want to have fun events and better than Disney Sundays. We want to see boys and girls, not just excited about church and learning about Jesus; but excited about walking in relationship with him, experiencing Jesus. It doesn't matter how big your VBS attendance was. It doesn't matter how amazing your facility is. It doesn't even matter how much money was raised for missions, or what crazy thing you have to do as a result (human sundae anyone?). What matters is that Jesus is at the center, not just the center of the programing, but at the center of the boys' and girls' hearts.

Our heartbeat and prayer are that the kids in your community and ministry will show up excited to have fun learning about Jesus and be passionate about experiencing him in their everyday life. We need Jesus at the core of what we do to accomplish this goal. Jesus. [period] during game time, small groups, snack time – all the time.

If you've been in kidmin for longer than 5 minutes, you know that there are struggles. Some days, kids don't listen and parents are difficult. There might be days when you want to throw in the towel or seasons where you try to coast through. On those days, in those seasons, remember the why. You aren't a glorified babysitter or fun factory. You are showing boys and girls the radical love of Jesus so they can experience him. Remember your why... Jesus. [period]

10

[LIVING IT OUT]

- *What is the why behind what you do?*

- *Would you say that Jesus is at the core of every aspect of your ministry?*

- *What specific areas of your ministry need more Jesus [period]?*

JESUS AND YOU
INFLUENCING FOR THE
LIFE-CHANGER

Beth Frank

[
But his delight is in the law of the Lord, and on his law he
meditates day and night.
-Psalm 1:2
]

Have you ever been "influenced"? Meaning you bought something
that you didn't even know you needed because someone on social
media told you that they absolutely couldn't live without it? Sometimes
I've been influenced and purchased items. Okay, I'll be honest, I've
purchased a lot of things I saw promoted on social media. Who knew
that a silicone strainer would be so convenient or that a nugget ice
machine would change my life? I never knew that I needed makeup
wipes in my nightstand till an influencer told me and now I can't
imagine not having them. Influencers can wield tremendous power over
our spending habits and even thought processes. Being an influencer

is now considered an actual job and people are making careers out of promoting lifestyles, products and brands on social media platforms.

What makes influencers so influencing? I've thought about this question a lot lately and of course I wanted to see what Google thought as well. Here's what I found on a Google search.

"Quality influencers know what makes their audiences tick. **They know how to entertain, how to engage, and how to persuade.** Good influencers also know how to tell a great story that captivates and convinces (plus, humans are generally predisposed to love a good narrative)."

I believe in addition to this Google answer, that influencers are the most alluring when they have used the product they are promoting and it has made their life better, easier or more enjoyable. They themselves are satisfied customers and that can't help but shine through the screen and grab our attention and wallets.

There is an old quote that I am not sure who said it originally, that goes something like "The best advertising a Christian can do is to be a satisfied customer themself." Really, as kid's pastors and volunteers our jobs are a lot like these social media influencers. We need to entertain, engage and persuade by telling the most captivating story of all time. We are influencing for the ultimate Life-Changer!

To influence on this level, I need to definitely be a satisfied customer myself. I need to know the captivating story of Jesus well. I need to have my own captivating story of how Jesus is working in my life today, not last year, not last season, not even last week, but today. How can we live like that kind of influencer. I can't possibly achieve that influencer status without first having Jesus at the very center of my own life. Does Jesus mean so much to me that I literally can't stop raving about Him to the audience He has given me? Is the story Jesus is telling with my life captivating and convincing those watching? Has my life been so radically changed that I feel desperate for others to experience the goodness and grace that I have?

You see Kidmin Leader, we are called to be influencers! On one hand it's awe inspiring and humbling that we would ever be called to the job of influencer for the God of the universe. The God who spoke planets into existence. The God who created us from the dust of the ground. The God who loved us so much He sent His only Son to die for us. How could I ever represent that to an unbelieving and desperate world?

On the other hand, this influencing job is not complicated and anyone can do it. I only need to eat, think, breathe, and live what I am constantly meditating on. Psalm 1:2 says, *"His delight is in the law of the Lord; and in his law doth he meditate day and night."* A key component to our job as influencers is to delight in God's words and be breathing them in and out, day and night.

Remember I said not complicated… I did not say easy. In today's culture it isn't easy to keep Jesus in the center. So many other things push and pull for that position. Our minds are tempted to replace Jesus with worry, criticism, fear, stress, to-do lists, spouses, kids, relational issues. Media bombards us with thoughts and emotions perpetually that all vie to be center in our mind and hearts.

At a time when it is the most difficult to keep Jesus at the center, it is also the time when it's more crucial than ever. The kids and families we serve are desperately looking for someone to engage, captivate, and persuade them. We have access to about anything in the world in the palm of our hands with our phones. Teens and even kids today can try and engage in behavior at early ages because of their phones. Even just a decade ago kids were more protected just because of the simple fact of access. Now phones are an all-access pass to filling the God void in a young person's life. If you are lonely, try to cultivate friends and likes on social media. If you are scared you don't have a purpose, try a dating app where someone will value you for the way you look. If you have been hurt numb your mind to the pain with binging Netflix. If you are craving sexual intimacy then look at porn. There is literally no end to the access or what people can try today in their desperate search. The heartbreaking thing about this search is that it always takes you further down into what you are trying to escape from, things like fear, anxiety, shame, guilt, loneliness, and uselessness. Further from the TRUTH. Only Jesus is the answer to this search. He is the Life-Changer. Are our lives reflecting that?

I believe so many teens and tweens are deconstructing from the faith today not because our teaching methods are lacking. I think the problem is we as leaders are not living as satisfied customers. We are attempting to influence without showing how the product is working for us. If the children and teens we serve see us searching and living unfulfilled lives apart from grace they will never want what we have. We can't captivate and engage disconnected from the power source. Methods aren't the answer for today's generation of young disciples. New or different programming isn't going to save the kids in our churches and communities. Do we really think we have lost a generation of kids because of teaching methods? Kids don't care so much about what we know, they care about what we do and how we live. If Jesus is real and powerful in my life as a leader then my kids will see this. If I am experiencing and raving about His grace and radical life change then the little people around me can't help but be captivated.

There is someone in the Bible that experienced real life change and that life change definitely captivated the hearts and minds of generations to come. As Kidmin leaders I am sure you are familiar with II Kings 22 and the young King of Judah, Josiah. Sunday School teachers love to tell the story of the king who came to the throne at the young age of 8. Josiah's father and grandfather had not worshipped God, but Josiah himself had to make a decision to worship the one true God.

II Kings tells the account of 18 years into Josiah's reign when he sends money to fix up the temple. While this is being accomplished the Book of Law is found and brought to Josiah. Many Bible scholars believe this was the book of Deuteronomy written by Moses. As Josiah reads, he realizes that Judah has indeed sinned deeply. Josiah doesn't waste a minute and calls the people of Judah to listen as the Book of Law is read aloud for all to hear. Can you imagine it? For the first time in your life standing with your family and friends and hearing God's words to His people being read aloud. I am sure there would have been awe and wonder at hearing from God like this, but also the guilt and shame over Judah's history of sin. As more words were read the people would have had a growing certainty that things needed to change and they need to change now.

Josiah repents along with many people. Josiah's repentance is shown by how he immediately goes into action. He burns all of the vessels made for Baal worship outside the city. He commands for all alters and high places to be torn down. He destroyed chariots dedicated to the worship of the sun. He also renewed the celebration of Passover like Moses had described it in the Book of Law. Josiah did not let the words of truth just sit in his mind and think on them. No, the words from the book of law captivated and spurred him to radical change. He wasn't content with the status quo anymore, he wanted to do all that God had said.

Josiah's reign was not as long as his grandfathers, but his influence was far superior. The Bible has high praise for Josiah in II Kings 23:25 *"Neither before nor after Josiah was there a king like him who turned to the Lord as he did — with all his heart and with all his soul and with all his strength, in accordance with all the Law of Moses."*

It is amazing to think about Josiah and his heart for God when you consider he had an evil grandfather and father and came to power at the very young age of 8 while living in a culture the was inundated with idols and the worship of them. When you read the verse in light of the context of Josiah's life you understand that this was a man that decided from an early age to prioritize keeping God at the center of all He did.

His life is marked by a passionate pursuit of holiness. If God's word said it, He wanted to obey it.

There is no doubt that Josiah's life had influence. He influenced an entire country into repentance. Despite Josiah being a Godly king, God's anger against Judah was still kindled and He was still going to judge the country and a lot of that had to do with Josiah's grandfather, Manasseh (II Kings 23:26). That may leave some of us wondering how "successful" was Josiah's influence. Ah, but we haven't got to my favorite part of this story yet.

Remember in the 18th year of Josiah's reign when he gathered all the people together for the reading from the book of the law? Remember how we were imaging what that must have felt like to be there on that day. How life-changing of an event it would have been hearing God's words read corporately. Even if you didn't get to be there in person that day, I'm sure word of what happened and the reaction of the people spread far and wide quickly.

The Book of Law was the standard for what God expected of His chosen people. There were possibly some very special parents in the crowd that day. Some parents that when they heard the word of the Lord read aloud, they fell in love with God all over again. Maybe their commitment to Him and His ways was renewed that day. All we know is that Josiah's influence and commitment to Scripture must have had a profound effect. And I believe it had a trickle-down affect to the parents of 5 special boys. Daniel, Hananiah, Mishael, Azariah and Ezekiel were probably all about the same age to within just a few years and we can learn from different Scripture passages that they would have been born around the 18th year of Josiah's reign.

These five young men were raised by parents who passed their love of Yahweh onto them. Little did Josiah or these parents know what all of these five boys would face in their lifetimes. Daniel, Hananiah, Mishael, Azariah and Ezekiel are an example of what we want for our kids today. They knew what they believed and could live their beliefs even in captivity in a pagan culture. I have a small picture hanging in a place where I am reminded to pray for my girls. The picture is rendering of what it might have been on the day that Hananiah, Mishael, Azariah faced the idol and the decision of whether to bow or not. Some of us know them better by their Babylonian names of Shadrach, Meshech, and Abidego. The picture shows thousands of people bowing before an idol and the three friends standing alone. Standing alone knowing they were facing certain death. Standing facing not only death, but death in a fiery furnace. My heart for my girls is summed up in that one picture. I pray they would always stand for Jesus in the face of whatever comes their way. Whenever I look at the picture, I think of an old 90's song by 4Him called Future Generations. The chorus says,

"We won't bend and we won't break, we won't water down our faith, we won't compromise in a world of desperation, what has been we cannot change, for tomorrow and today, we must be a light for future generations."

This song and this picture should be our anthem for the kids and the families in our ministries. Keep standing.

We all know our culture in increasingly hostile to Jesus and His words. Realistically this is what our kids our facing right now. The kids in our ministries hear the truth proclaimed on Sundays and hopefully from their Jesus-loving parents but then they enter a world that is standing in many ways in complete opposition to the truth they just heard. What will happen when a friend, teacher, coach, book, news cast, TV show, movie, song, celebrity, athlete, magazine article, or social post tells them a different "truth". Will they bend? How can we help them stand in a sea of complacency and compromise.

What does it take to produce a faith that doesn't bend? It requires strength to stand. Strength that comes from muscles built up over time. Again, I want to interject Psalm 1:2, *"His delight is in the law of the Lord, and on his law he meditates day and night."* Every single day our kids need truth. They need to see it applied and how that impacts our life and theirs as well. I can't walk into a gym and immediately be able to go and lift weights that someone who has been training and working out for years is able to. It takes time, hard work, and sweat to build the muscle. This is why it is so important for kids to be able to flex their truth muscles starting at a young age. When we are meditating on the word it is constantly on our mind and lips. How can we give kids truth with handles on it? A take home paper with the week's Bible verse just isn't going to cut it. Our kids need to see scripture at work in their life. If what I teach on Sunday is relevant and able to be put to use on Monday my kids will be able to grow their truth muscles. Truth in action is powerful. The people in Josiah's day experienced that when the truth was read and then change resulted from that. Obedience was the key to influence. Our kids will be influenced in a powerful way when we can help them to experience truth in action.

How can we ever hope to produce Daniels, Hananiahs, Mishaels, Azariahs and Ezekiels? The same way Josiah did. By delighting in the law of the Lord so much that our own lives are radically changed. When we delight in something we love it and happily go along with whatever that something requires. It is easy to obey something I am delighted about. It is easy change for something that I am enamored with. When I delight in something it easily dictates my responses. If you think about it, our responses to people and situations expose who we really are. Just like our kid's responses expose who they really are. When we are faced with challenges or problems do we bend, do we cave or do we respond with scripture. The only possible way to respond with scripture is if Psalm 1:2 is a reality in my life and the lives of the kids I am serving. Our kids should have a front row seat to see all that God is doing. God is moving mightily in this generation, don't let our kids miss it. Bring every single of their joys, frustrations, accomplishments, problems, and responses, every single aspect of their lives back to scripture. Jesus. [period] in every situation and response.

Being an Influence now isn't just about the here and now. Josiah had no idea when he read the Book of Law and radically obeyed all that it said how he was influencing generations to come. Hananiah, Mishael, Azariah would stand in the face of a fiery furnace, Daniel would pray in the face of the lion's den, and Ezekiel would lead the rebuilding of Jerusalem. We have no idea this side of eternity what our influence truly is. Keep Jesus in the center of everything and keep being an influencer for the true Life-Changer, Jesus. [period]

LIVING IT OUT

- *What can you do this week to grow closer to God yourself?*

- *How can you pray for your kids as they enter a spiritually hostile world each day?*

- *How can you do a better job putting handles on what you teach each week?*

JESUS AND YOUR KIDS

WALKING IN THE LIGHT

Hannah Bolvi

[
I am the light of the world. Whoever follows me will never
walk in darkness, but will have the light of life.
-John 8:12
]

The year that it hit me, there were eight graduating seniors.

As we listened to the seniors talk about the things that they had
learned in youth group, there was one question that I couldn't ignore:
where are the rest? This group of graduating youth group seniors had
been part of a class that was once nearly 35 strong. Where were the rest
of them?

Sure, some of them had moved away. Some of them had faced life
circumstances that had taken them away but... not all...so what about
the rest?

The reality is that many of them had left the church because they were old enough to stay home and sleep in on a Sunday morning. They were old enough to decide for themselves if they wanted to come on Wednesday night... So why weren't they here, standing with their peers and talking about Jesus?

Had we failed them? Had we dropped the ball? Not been fun enough? Cool enough? Too many cliques? Was an Old Testament study the wrong choice?

And then, in a still-small-voice that shot through my heart like a bolt of lightning, the answer came.

If they're not here, it's because they didn't find something worth coming back for.

What do you mean, Lord? We were teaching the truth, trying to make it fun, and we had programs and activities to engage the entire family in multiple ways... we were doing all of the right things.

Still-small-Voice:

> *Had we really shown them what it feels like to be head over heels in love with Jesus?*
> *Had we really shown them what it looks like to be enamored with the character of God?*
> *Had we really shown them that God alone is good and 'apart from him we have no good thing'?*
> *Had we shown them that there was nothing in this world that would satisfy the longing in their souls like Jesus?*
> *...Was I fully convinced that nothing in this world would satisfy the longing in MY soul like Jesus?*

Sure. Yes.

Of course I did.

In theory… but did I really?

If you looked at my choices, what would the evidence from my life lead you to believe?

We can't sell what we don't have. And we can't buy with currency that we haven't earned. Jesus.[period] Was going to have to start with me…

I grew up in church. I mean that literally. I was a pastor's kid, so I was there all the time. Not just for church services. There were calling and visitation nights; we were early for choir practice and we would stay late for special events. As a matter-of-course I could always be found at VBS, AWANA, church-run summer day camp, Christmas Cantatas, Easter Passion plays, Fourth of July celebrations, Missions Weeks, special speaker events, conferences, weddings, funerals… oh, and did I mention that I went to the Christian school attached to the church? I grew up IN the church.

I knew all the things, and had all the answers by heart. I sang the hymns and helped clean up the little plastic cups after communion. I gave my heart to Jesus at five, and was baptized at seven. My parents were faithful to talk about hard things. They were honest about their own struggles and how much they needed Jesus. I was shielded from some of the childhood burnout that so many pastors' kids face because of their careful shepherding. But deep underneath the surface there was a contract being written in my own heart. A contract that said, "I do all the things right and then You, God, in turn give me a good life," or in more church-y terms: "I commit my way to the Lord and then MY plans will succeed."

The root of the problem was that I was developing a silent, hidden theology that the goodness of God was proven by my life circumstances.

That God was good because I could see His goodness in my life. He was good, and he promised me that if I obey and make certain lifestyle sacrifices, then he would protect me and those that I loved. Oh, 16 year old self, you had so much to learn.

Within a few short years trials and challenges would come, forcing me to confront my deep-seated misconceptions about the goodness of God. Trials that would bring me face-to-face with the truth: that my transactional theology, the deal that I thought I had made with God, was not sturdy enough to stand against the realities of life in the fallen world.

20 years old: *Heart hollow, soul shattered. Expectations dashed. "God are you there? How did I get here? To this place? I thought I did everything right. I thought I followed the map. I married the one voted most likely to be a mega church pastor. How could I have known he was a wolf in sheep's clothing? YOU knew. Why didn't you warn me? Warn someone?! Why didn't you protect me from this? Will I ever be worthy of love again? Will I ever be qualified to serve you again? Or, will I wear a scarlet letter of abuse, abandonment and divorce all my life? Oh God, I am only twenty years old, how did I get here? All I wanted was to serve you..."*

28 years old: *I am empty inside. In.every.way. "There was no heartbeat on the ultrasound Father." Again. We have already been here before. I don't want to walk this road again. I can't keep bearing only loss and death. I can't keep nursing only grief. You give and you take away, that is for sure, but I am not ready to praise you in this yet. My heart feels as dead as the baby inside my body. You know I love kids. I WORK WITH KIDS IN MINISTRY. Why would you not allow us to become parents? What is wrong with me? IS THERE SOMETHING wrong with me?*

30 years old: *Low-burning anger and the slow trickle of grief that comes before the loss... the dripping away of a loved one like the dripping IVs of the chemo bags. Father it's back. The Doctors say we can't operate this time. It's too dangerous. It's growing too fast. God help us. She is so young. They have*

only been married for a little over a year. My sweet sister. It's not fair. It's too much… grief upon grief.

Do you know what it means to be ugly-honest? The kind of honest-with-your-own-soul to the point that you don't necessarily like what you see. The kind of honest that you would hate for others to catch a glimpse of. The part with the burning questions and the doubts. Who you really are under all of the layers of glossy right answers and the breezy refrains of worship songs you sing beside neighbors at church.

I love/hate/love ugly-honest. Ugly-honest is the only place where I can begin to see what holds me down and, ugly-honest is where I can start to find freedom. It is the place where the Lord can help me to *"Lay aside every sin that entangles and every weight that hinders"* so that I can then *"run with endurance the race marked out before me"*. Ugly-honest is hard. But if you feel heavy and burdened, embracing the ugly-honest truth is one of the steps that begin to move you in the direction of grace. Until you *know* who you are, you *cannot* accept the truth that re-defines you and sets you free. Until you look in the mirror (James 1) and take note of how you look, you cannot begin to fix the things that may already be obvious to others and are certainly already obvious to God. Ugly-honest is where I started to see the cracks in my own private theology of the goodness of God. Ugly-honest is where the start of true freedom is found.

We have to look at what our actual behavior says about our real desires. Most of us who have been in church all our lives are often so conditioned to give the churchy "right" answers that we can find it difficult to get beyond those knee-jerk responses, even if we are having a discussion with just our own hearts or journaling alone! We silence the voice of doubt before the thought can even form in our minds. We hush-up our own heart-hurt-questions before the thoughts crystallize. We are so afraid to look. Afraid to truly see the contents of our own souls. Afraid of what monsters might be hiding in the dark. I think I am, in a way, still afraid of the dark.

The other day my friend told me that "Disappointment is when our hearts have an appointment with something in the future and it disappears." Oh how easily I can attach my soul to things that don't exist! To futures that are castles-in-the-clouds of my own imagination. Imaginary castles are great for playing, but my soul needs a more solid foundation. And if I was going to grow past my made-up theology and my imaginary gospel I was going to have to flip on the flashlight, take a deep breath and look in all of the corners. Ugly or not, here I come.

31 years old:

My Plans/Dreams/Expectations

To work a job I like for as long as I want a job... and then not have to work when I decide to retire or when I want to stay home.

To be happily married to someone who is healthy and whole.

To have healthy children, when we want them and how I want them to be born.

For us to have jobs that fulfill our passions, offer flexibility, and allow us to live comfortably- without consuming our lives.

To entertain.

To have a great house.

To pay bills, debt, and save for the future.

To be able to travel occasionally.

To have people think well of me.

To have a healthy family and healthy me- without much personal effort.

To have nice things.

To have two working cars- that are not ugly.

To feel like I matter/have purpose.

To breathe air, have my heart beat, walk, listen and speak without thinking about it.

To know that God loves me, and to feel ok, even when I don't read His Word, talk to Him, or obey.

To feel warm and fuzzy when I sing.

To be around in a year to write another list.

Lord, I choose to give You this list -My dreams/plans/ expectations.

I want to keep them. I want to control my future, but I know that I can't and I don't. I choose to give this to You because You know best and You are sovereign. Lord help me to trust you, help me to seek Your face.

I pray for/toward all of these things, but I trust You to do what is best. You have more than proven that Your ways are not my ways, and that in the end Your ways are best. I need You. I need Your help. Strengthen me and lead me.

Amen

At 31 years old, and for perhaps the first time, I realized that the real monster in the dark was me. I was the control monster who wanted to base God's goodness on my definition of good. Base it on His ability to follow MY plan. The truth was that I had little-to-no-control over whether I would get what I wanted. I could not resolve to "do better" and thereby earn the life I wanted. I could only ask God for His best according to His definition of goodness.

I think so many of us have this secret belief that a God who does things solely for His own glory is at the core, some kind of egotistical maniac... I know. Even putting that on paper seems like fire should come down from Heaven and consume this book like Elijah's altar.

BUT IT'S TRUE.

We have this quiet, discontented feeling that God is always looking out for His own interests, even if that is at the expense of OUR good. And that we are somehow supposed to be okay with that, because He is GOD and He is worthy.

There is one big problem with this theory.

That it looks nothing like Jesus.

When you read the Gospels you simply don't see it. Jesus is anything but egotistical, and Jesus is the EXACT representation of the Father. We never hear Him say or do anything that even hints at a this-is-going-to-hurt-you-more-than-it-hurts-me,-but-it's-okay-because-I-am-GOD attitude. In fact, we see the opposite.

Jesus humbled Himself. He was marked by His HUMILITY, not His ego. He humbled Himself and became obedient to death, even death on a cross. The cross and resurrection are the ultimate definition of who God IS. Every other thought must be shadowed and filtered by this one idea. Jesus came humbly, to live, to show us who God is. He died a physically brutal - but so much more spiritually brutal - death when He took on all of the sin of the world. Take a moment to take that in.

HE took upon HIMSELF the sin of the world.

Imagine the sin in this moment.

The anger being spouted online and in homes, the war, the abuse, the greed, the selfish ambition in the world right now, this very second.

The weight of every lie being spoken, of the pride dismantling justice, of all the coveting and adultering and lusting occurring just in this one moment.

Jesus took the shame and wrath and heaviness of all of that.

All of it; and not just in this moment, but in every generation, back to the first bite of pride and up to the final word spat in anger before Jesus comes back. He took it all on His own body on the tree. So that when He defeated death just days later, we would be able to sing with full-throated voice "sin has no claim on me" and mean it.

God is not an egotist.

No way.

The cross proves that.

Why then does this lie that God's glory is somehow selfish remain so pervasive?

The problem lies with our understanding of the word GLORY. Glory can be defined as the visual representation of the character or nature of a person, place or thing. Or the things that make it unique or lovely. So the "glories of Paris" are the things that make Paris unique and lovely. The glories of a flower are its color, shape, position in a landscape, its smell and transient beauty.

God's glory is HIS character and attributes on display. It is His justice and mercy. His love and compassion. His patience and His wrath for soul-destroying-sin. His glory is His ability to be ever with us, His way of meeting us right where we are and speaking directly to our very hurt. We see His glory in the way He has of winning us with kindness and calling us to holiness for our own freedom and good. So, more of God's glory on the earth means there is more love being shown to the lonely. More glory is more joy on the faces of the young and old. More glory is more justice for displaced and vulnerable peoples. More glory is more hope for the discouraged or grieving. More glory is more peace in homes, churches and schools. It's more wrongs-made-right, and more light-from-darkness. This is glory.

You know what this means? It means that when God allows hard things to happen, they ARE for His own glory. The thing is, His glory is what our *souls crave*. The hard things give us the opportunity to experience God in a way we would otherwise never see, feel or even imagine.

We crave peace and calling, and that is what he inexplicably gave me in the middle of the nightmare of a broken and abusive relationship and in the healing after …as well as grace in the time of learning to trust someone else later. That is glory. That's who He is.

We crave an anchor for our souls, and He showed me that He is the only firm place to stand when we had our second miscarriage. He also used that season to deepen and strengthen our marriage. God used my husband in that season, who faithfully helped me hold on to truth when I was too weak. Now in year 18 of our marriage, we thank God for that hard season because He was there and it was a huge growing time for us. We felt His faithful presence so close. That is glory. That's who He is.

We crave hope and belonging, and He surrounded us with love and community in the season where we walked through the loss of my sister. Those months deepened our longing for heaven and home. That is glory. That's who He is.

I have often said of the hard seasons of my life that I would not have chosen them, but now that I am on the other side, I would not go back and change them if I could. They were invaluable in shaping who I am today. Jesus's glory is often seen most clearly in a storm; when against all reason, He stands up and says "peace be still," and either the waves calm or we do. We can't know deep peace anywhere else. We crave love that never leaves, so Jesus went to the cross to show us that there is a love that will cross any barrier or boundary, even death, to be with us. That is glory.

It is not wrong to say that God allows hard things for His glory. He does. God also allows hard things for my greatest good. Any loving parent gets this idea. I don't want my child to experience pain, but growing can be painful and I would never choose to halt their growth. Where is the reason to doubt God is good when He allows pain to help us find true freedom and fullness of joy?

Every desire that I have is at its core a heart cry for glory.

A few weeks ago in my discipleship group, as an exercise, we wrote out what we wanted most in life right now. Then we looked at its roots, at the desire under the desire.

We found all of our desires boiled down to the same basic things:

- Homes, good jobs, financial stability —> Security, deeper roots, sense of home
- Spouses, kids, community, close friends —> Love, approval, acceptance, belonging
- Worry-free, Whole and healed life, —> uninhibited joy, comfort, abundance, pleasure
- Restored relationships, reunion with loved ones —> Redemption of brokenness and loss
- Working in our passion area, using our gifts —> Eternal purpose and deeper meaning

All of these things at the root are good. We rarely have moments where we experience them all at once. They are all found only in tastes and sips on earth, but in full and hearty abundance in heaven. Through our desires, God is whetting our appetite for heaven and home -which of course is full of the glory of the Lord.

Heaven is the place where the root of our desires is found, and it is the only place we will truly feel full and at home

When I feast on the goodness of God and His work on the cross, when I look at my life through the lens of a proper theology of glory, and not my self-made theology, I find freedom. My heart fills with gratitude and love for His goodness and mercy and love. I want to hum worship songs in the car. My eyes start to sparkle when I talk about His love, and my lashes get damp when I think about heaven. My soul fills with a deep sense of longing and a lump forms in my throat.

Those are the moments we need our kids to see. That is why they should come back. That is the real thing worth returning for. It's not a formula. Love demands free will. Love must be chosen, but the glory of love has a siren song in all of us.

The challenge is that a belief in God's goodness is not a commodity that can be ordered online. It's not in a curriculum pack. It doesn't come with crafts. It must start with a deep personal experience of God. A welcoming of the work of the Spirit. A willingness to look back and revisit past heartache, in search of the glory that you might have missed in the hard moments. It can't be faked, manufactured or rushed.

Especially with kids. Kids are willing to believe almost anything, but they have a deep "spidey-sense" for the inauthentic. Kids will love broken people much faster than they will welcome a fake. It's a God-given x-ray vision. And if you don't pass the test - if they can sense that you don't really, fully believe what you are teaching - then you will lose them. So do you?

It doesn't matter how cool, creative, and fun your lessons are; if kids don't see the soul-changing power of the cross at work in your life, they will walk away. And they won't even truly understand what they are walking away from.

My prayer for the kids that walked away is that God will get a hold of them, show them what they missed, and bring them back.

My prayer for us today is that we don't lose anyone else... starting with you. The teens are not the only ones leaving. Life in ministry can be tough. You too need a firm grasp on glory to make it week after week in the real world of ministry. You need peace and calling... and grace to stick with it when no one shows up to help. You need an anchor in the storm when things get messy with leadership. You need hope and belonging as you seek to create a community that is counter culture and gives kids a real glimpse of who God truly is. You need Jesus. [period]

| LIVING IT OUT |

- *Am I showing the kids in my ministry what it feels like to be head over heels in love with Jesus?*

- *How am I helping the kids in my ministry with their ugly-honest truth and seeing glory in all their situations?*

- *What are things that could be holding your ministry kids back from truly believing in the goodness of God? What dark corners need to be illuminated with truth?*

JESUS IN EVERYTHING

INTENTIONALITY AND FUN

Amber Pike

[
All Scripture is God-breathed and is useful for teaching,
rebuking, correcting and training in righteousness.
-2 Timothy 3:16
]

Why do you do what you do? For most all of us serving in kidmin, we were called to serve. While we know that God doesn't <u>need</u> us to lead boys and girls to the Kingdom, he lets us help grow his Kingdom. Serving in kidmin isn't something that we have to do, but rather something that we <u>get</u> to do. Quite literally, it's the best job ever!

Week in and week out, as kidmin leaders, we get to share the love of Jesus to boys and girls. We teach about the life-changing love of Jesus & make the word of God come alive. Sometimes we have the honor of seeing a child grow in their faith during their years in our ministry. Watching one of your babies accept Christ as their Lord and Savior is one of the best feelings in the world! But not all children remain in our ministry (or our church even) for those 6-8 years of childhood. Some children may remain for just a season of their lives. Other children may visit occasionally; while others still visit for just one Sunday.

Think about that child – the child you had for just one hour.

Did you use your hour well?

In 2019, the average church-going child was in church for about 2 hours a month. I have kids that I see maybe one Sunday a month. One hour a month, 12 hours a year, isn't much time to teach them about Jesus. Every single minute counts. We need to be intentional about using every hour, every minute that children are in our church to point them to Jesus. [period]

Once upon a time, children's ministry was commonly viewed as a need – a way to keep the kids entertained so the real learning could take place for the adults in the sanctuary. And while the kids are there, they could have a Bible story being read to them, given a coloring page to work on, and a snack. It was basically babysitting. But we aren't babysitters. There is no junior faith or bite sized Gospel. Young children (preschool age, even) are capable of great understanding and legitimate salvation and relationship with Christ.

How do we make sure that we are doing more than just babysitting? Kidmin is about Jesus. [period]. And it takes intentionality in everything we do.

HAVE A PLAN.

What do you want the kids in your ministry to know by the time they leave children's ministry and enter into youth ministry? Do you even have a goal?

Just like a budget tells your money where it should go, your curriculum should be used to tell the level of learning where to go. You need to have a plan for your ministry!

You could just pick out a variety of curriculum that appeals to you – maybe you like the decorations, or you really want to teach on Joseph again, or you didn't have time to prep a lesson so you're picking something easy. Without a plan, will your kids, by the time they leave your ministry, have a solid view of God and the Bible? Will their relationship with him be strong and their lives showing fruit?

For some kids, church is the only Jesus they see. Mom and dad might not be shepherding, so you need to make sure your lessons are teaching to the full extent.

Kids need to know who God is.

- They need to know the meta-narrative of the Bible (God's story of redemptive love for his creation).
- Kids need to know that they are sinners and only Jesus can forgive their sins and give them the gift of eternal life.
- They need to know what it looks like to grow in their faith and walk in relationship with God.

Don't just hope all of this (and more) gets taught and caught over the course of a child's time in your ministry. It needs to be intentionally taught over and over. If the goal is seeing resilient, lifelong followers of Christ, your curriculum is the tool to help this become a reality.

HAVE A PURPOSE.

Do you have a reason for doing the things you do in your lessons and ministry? Why did you plan that particular game? Why was that event scheduled or that resource sent home? With the realization in mind that we have a limited amount of hours to pour into our kids, we need to be planning with a purpose in mind.

Every minute can (and should) be intentional!

How can you be intentionally pouring into kids before service?
Instead of just letting kids hang out, how can you use these minutes to grow children in their faith? Is there music and/or a video that can be played in the background to help hide God's Word in their hearts? Maybe leaders can be running games or activities to work on Bible skills or introduce the day's lesson.

Can snack time be used to grow kids in their faith?
Much to the dismay of my kids, I did away with snack time at our church. For us, it took up too much time. Someone always wanted more, at least 3 kids spilled something that needed cleaning up, and there was always a child or two who ate slowly and couldn't participate in the next activity. I wanted those precious minutes back, so I took snack time away. (And yes, there was much grumbling.) Now when we have a snack, there's a purpose behind it.

While teaching on Elisha wanting a double portion of Elijah's spirit, kids had the opportunity to get a double portion of whipped cream on their pudding.

An ice cream sundae event (with all the mix-ins you can think of) becomes an illustration on how putting God into our lives changes us.

Birthday cake helps us celebrate the birth of the Savior.

Snacks don't have to happen every week. (Sometimes it's more special when it's not regular). But they can be used to bring the lesson home and make it stick in the minds of boys and girls.

Do the games you play have a purpose?

Dodgeball is by far the most favorite and requested game during VBS. If I let them, the teens would lead the kids in doing nothing but playing dodgeball. But I won't. While fun, dodgeball at VBS, needs to have a purpose. Games need a purpose.

Now, sometimes the purpose might be just to get some wiggles out. (We have all been there!) But I challenge you to go a step further than just planning games to get wiggles out. With a little creativity and intentionality, games can be used to teach, introduce, or review your lesson. The game itself might not be "spiritual" – not every game has to be Bible trivia or super themed (like Daniel and the Lion's Den tag). A game might be a regular, fun game. The challenge is in intentionally tying it to the lesson.

- Jailbreak tag can lead into the story of Paul and Silas in prison.
- Freeze tag can intro the account of the 4 friends that brought their friend to Jesus.
- Red Light Green Light can illustrate the Great Commission.

Kids learn through games and play! Not only are they learning social skills and teamwork while moving their bodies, but kids actually retain more while their bodies are moving. Lots of research shows a link between the physical and the cognitive. When their bodies are involved, up and moving, kids can learn and retain better. Be intentional with those games!

Are your purposefully giving kids the opportunity to apply God's Word to their lives and respond?

Church should be more than just hearing stories about God. Children need to know their role in God's story. They need to experience God!

What is his word telling them? How does the day's lesson apply to their lives? What action steps should they be taking?

Are they being invited to see the transformational power of prayer?

Are kids being challenged to worship beyond just "doing motions?"

Kids can most definitely apply God's Word to their lives. But they are still kids. On their own, they might not be able to make those connections. After a lesson on Aaron and the golden calf, children might not naturally make the leap to prayerfully discover if they have placed idols in their lives like an adult might. This is where intentionality comes in. With the activities and format of your lesson, how can you give kids the opportunity to respond and apply while at church? How can this habit translate to the home?

In every area of your ministry, ask yourself, what is the purpose? Why are you doing it? Keep the goal in mind of pouring into your kids so that you might see lifelong followers of Christ. Are you intentionally pointing kids to Jesus [period]?

HAVE FUN.

Yep. I said it. Have fun! Kidmin should be fun! We are working with kids! There should be laughter, silliness, and excitement. Don't be afraid to get a little silly (maybe even dress a little crazy). Fun should be standard in your ministry. They are kids. They need fun!

This doesn't mean, however, that everything single thing at church has to be full of fun and crazy silliness. There is a time and place for quiet and serious. Fun can look different, as well. It's not all jumping up and down screaming. My Sunday school class isn't full of games and silliness. It's a small group of kids, and we sit around the table with God's Word. But it's fun. (How do I know? One of my kids actually told me this recently.) I pour into my kids. I build the relationships with them. And because I am excited about the Word of God, about teaching the lesson, it makes it fun for them.

Church should be fun. Kids should want to be there, because learning about Jesus is fun! When kids aren't having fun, do you know what happens? They get bored.

- When kids are bored, they start acting up (or out).
- When kids are bored, they check out mentally and stop paying attention.
- When kids are bored, they stop wanting to come.

Boredom is a real danger in ministry. (I was that kid! I loved Jesus, but I when I was bored in youth group, I acted up!) Making church fun isn't the same thing as simply entertaining children, though. Make it fun by engaging kids.

Make things fun by giving kids more.
Kids are capable of a really high level of learning. Oftentimes, it's higher than we think. We need to be challenging kids to learn more, kidmin leaders. Are they going to understand and retain every detail you teach them? Absolutely not! But are they going to be further in their faith knowledge if you give them more rather than less? You betcha!

Keep in mind that not all kids learn at the same level. Some children have a higher level of understanding about their faith, even already following Christ at a young age, while others might not be there yet. In a room full of children all the same age, you will have a variety of learning and comprehension levels. That's ok. Since kids developmentally are at different levels, and they mature at different rates; we need to be intentional in reaching different levels of learning. Plus, kids will rise to the level you set for them. If you only set the bar so high, that's as high as they will reach. Set the bar higher. Teach kids more. Challenge them to learn and grow more… you just might be surprised.

Can you teach preschoolers that God is omnipotent? Absolutely! (And make sure you're using the word!) Are all kids going to remember this one hundred percent? Maybe, maybe not. But if you are intentionally and repetitively teaching them more, giving them theology and using those big words; they will learn it and retain it.

When kids are underfed – boredom creeps in and they disengage. Give them more. Teach more than just stories. Teach the narrative of the Bible and theology. Use those big words!

While you are giving them more (and deeper) biblical content…

Make things fun for all children by engaging all learning styles and smarts.
Not all kids learn in the same way. If you teach each lesson using just one or two learning styles, a lot of kids are missing out.

- Just speaking the lesson only reaches the auditory learners.
- Visual learners need to see it in front of them. (That's me, I'm a visual learner).
- Kinesthetic learners need to do it and touch something to learn. (My son is more kinesthetic).

These are the three big learning styles that you are probably familiar with. And honestly, it's pretty easy to do all three in every lesson. You can speak the lesson (auditory). Then kids can read a passage out of the Bible or read text on the screens (visual). You can then play a game or do an activity to reinforce it (kinesthetic). You just reached all three types in one lesson. That is great, but you can (and should) strive for more.

The goal is to have boys and girls learning about Jesus and developing a lifelong relationship with him – all boys and girls.

Even the kids who learn through music.

Or art.
Or math.
Or writing.
Or nature.
Or through their peers.
Or even self-learners.

(Are you getting the idea?)

While you teach, your goal needs to be incorporating as many of these different learning styles and smarts as possible, all in the same lesson. When you do, you are maximizing your teaching. You are reaching the greatest number of kids with the highest level of retention.

Let's say we are talking about David praising God. If the lesson is being spoken, auditory learners are engaged. When you add in pictures and text on the screen, visual learners are engaged. For music-smart kids, you can have kids sing a praise song, adding in scarves or shaky eggs for kids who need to move. Have kids write their own praise songs (word-smart kids will love this). But give kids the option to work in groups (for the peer-smart kids) or individually (for self-learners). And don't forget that not all kids can write, so give them the option to draw their praises to God (good for art-smart kids or younger kids who can't write yet).

That's a lot! That's a lot of planning, too. But with the intentionality put into that lesson, you just engaged multiple children in multiple ways... in ways that will stick with them. Because they had fun learning in a way (or ways) that make sense to their brains, they will remember it better.

Make things fun by getting kids moving!

If you were really honest, you'd probably admit that even as a grown up, you have more fun and are more engaged when you aren't sitting in the same spot for a really long time. The same is true for kids. When kids are sitting still too long, they unengage and start to zone out. Or talk. Or misbehave. Or "need" to go to the bathroom several times. Sometimes to re-engage kids, they just need to move.

Have a 10 second wiggle break. Truly, that 10 seconds of moving their bodies can refocus their attention. While a wiggle break or dance party can help refocus kids, kids actually learn better through movement.

Use motions or sign language to help memorize verses (through song or just through memory).

Solidify the lesson's point by adding motions to phrases kids say.

Have kids go to a different spot for the next portion of the lesson.

Movement is a huge tool when you teach to keep kids engaged in the lesson and the Word, plus it makes things more fun.

Do a quick little assessment and see if your ministry is fun. Are kids excited to come to church? Are they engaged in the lesson/activity/event?

- *Are you making the Word of God exciting?*
- *Are you engaging the children through a variety of senses?*
- *Have you used different teaching styles to engage multiple children?*
- *Do the leaders and volunteers seem happy and excited for kids to be there?*

Jesus isn't boring. Church shouldn't be boring. Be intentional to make church fun, and invite kids into Jesus' story and into relationship with him.

HAVE TIME SET ASIDE.

If the ultimate goal is to see kids walking with Jesus, we need to evaluate to see if the things we are doing in our ministry are helping accomplish that goal. The Holy Spirit is the one who does the work in the child's heart. As much as we wish it were up to us whether a child follows Christ or not, it isn't. It is up to God. There is no guarantee, no matter how awesome our lessons are or how much we love on kids, that they will walk in relationship with Christ. But, it is our job (what we have been called to do) to faithfully plant those seeds. To do our very best to **intentionally** point kids to Jesus [period]. Are you doing that well? Are you using that hour you have been given to its fullest extent?

We all get into patterns and rhythms that might not be our best. Life is busy. And sometimes, we like what is easiest. Raise your hand if you've ever waited to prep a lesson until the night before. (I'm going to guess a lot of hands are going up.) Or maybe you picked a curriculum simply because it was easiest on you and your team. But are those things truly helping you accomplish your goal (of seeing lifelong followers of Jesus)? This is why intentionality is so important, and intentionally (and regularly) evaluating is equally important.

Everything you do in ministry should be pointing kids to Jesus [period].

So, is it?

- Is the curriculum you are using engaging kids and teaching them Jesus' story?

- Are the events and activities that are planned furthering children's faith?
- Are families actively engaging in the resources being sent home, or are the resources simply more things on a to-do list that aren't getting done?
- Do children feel the love of Jesus as they walk through your doors from each and every team member?
- Are kids having fun and are they excited to be at church?
- Are you seeing children growing in their faith and bearing fruit?

Sit down with your team and take a hard look at just how intentional you are with your time. Think back to that child who came to your church for just one hour; one hour of his/her entire life. In those 60 minutes, those 3,600 seconds, what did you accomplish? Was it fun with a purpose? Was there love being poured out and the message of Jesus' saving grace being taught? Or was it just an hour of fun with a little bit of Jesus sprinkled in?

What you do each and every Sunday, with each event and every conversation, matters. One hour could make an eternal difference to a child.

Use your hour well. The devil is prowling, fighting for our kids. Eternity is at stake! Each and every minute we have with kids at church counts. Each and every lesson, every game, every conversation can make a difference. Be intentional. In everything you do, point boys and girls to Jesus [period].

[LIVING IT OUT]

- *Give yourself a quick rating. How well are you using your hour?*

- *How intentional are you in pointing kids to Jesus with each and every single thing you do?*

- *What areas do you need to work on being more intentional in?*

JESUS' WORDS
SCRIPTURE MEMORY, ISN'T THERE AN APP FOR THAT?
Natalie Abbott

[
Fix these words of mine in your hearts and minds...
-Deuteronomy 11:18a
]

If Jesus is the center of everything, shouldn't he be the center of our lives... and the lives of the kids in our ministry?

If Jesus is the owner of all things, if all things were made through him and he upholds them all by his powerful word, if he is the radiance of God's glory and the exact representation of the Father, if Jesus offered himself for our sins and now sits at the right hand of the Majesty in heaven (see Hebrews 1:2-4)... *If* all of this is actually true, *then* shouldn't he be the center of our lives and consequently our ministries? And all God's people said a hearty "YES and AMEN!"

But so often, Jesus isn't central, he's on the periphery.

This is going to sound strange, but Jesus is often overshadowed by all the Jesus-y things in our modern Christian lives and ministries. We have all the apps on our phones, follow all those godly influencers on Insta, and listen to all the podcasts and sermons on our commutes or when we fold laundry. We read all the Christian articles and books about justice, parenting, sexuality, and anxiety. We go to all the gospel-centered websites to answer our theological conundrums and practical Christian living questions. We work hard to find the best curriculum and to utilize the latest ministry resources in our ministries. Now, these are actually all good things, resources that ultimately are meant to point us to Jesus. But here's the tough question: have all the apps and trappings and Jesus-y things replaced Jesus at the center of our lives and the core of our ministries?

Ouch. Let's take inventory.

Are we spending more time doing Jesus-y things than we're spending with Jesus? Are we merely learning *about* Jesus or do we actually *know* Jesus? Are we mostly reading words about biblical ideas, or are we reading the Word of God? When we're worried, do we google Christian answers or do we go to Christ in prayer? Are we merely seeking to live rightly in our own strength or are we giving the Holy Spirit space to gently nudge us throughout our days? Are we mainly interacting with believers online or are we in real, face-to-face relationships with other Christians? Do kids in our church hear stories about our personal walk with God and the work He is doing in our lives? I know. That was a rapid-fire list of some pretty hard questions. At least, they're hard for me. Because, truth be told, I'm not happy with a lot of my answers. So often, all those Jesus-y things fill up my time—time I should be giving to Jesus himself.

So, how do we get back on track?

Scripture warns us that *"we must pay the most careful attention therefore to what we've heard, so that we will not drift away"* (Hebrews 2:1). Incidentally, this is the response given to all those statements about the supremacy of Christ that we looked at earlier. And here's the point: none of us wants to drift away, do we? We all want to live faithful, beautiful lives. But how? And this little verse has the answer: "we must pay the most careful attention" to Jesus. We must make him the center—the center of our lives and the center of our ministries to kids and families. When he is the center, all the noise and urgency of the world around us takes its proper place, at the periphery.

WHAT DOES THIS LOOK LIKE?

For me, I try to keep Jesus central by meditating on his Word throughout the day.

It might sound overly simple, but memorizing and dwelling on Scripture is the way I quiet my heart when it's pounding. Those words I've learned are the wisdom of God as I answer tough questions. They're the words I cling to when I wake up in a panic at 2 am. They're the praise on my lips when the sky turns cotton candy colors. Those words are how I respond to the horrors on the news. Most of all, those words tether me to Jesus as the hours pass and the days add up.

Let me give you a real-life example.

The other morning, out of nowhere, a flood of fear broke into my day. The enemy started whispering lies in my ear—really convincing lies, lies that sounded true. He said: I'm not good enough to do what God has for me. I don't write anything that matters. This ministry is too much. I'll never be able to do all of this and keep up with my ginormous family. I should probably find a replacement and quit. I'm dead serious here. My chest started to feel tight and my lungs felt flat. Truth be told, this is not an unusual scenario. So, I did what I've trained myself to do in these moments. I sat down right then and there, and I prayed. And do you know what came to my mind? Scripture. I prayed this verse right back to God: *"The Spirit you gave me does not make me timid, but gives me power, love and self-discipline."* (from 2 Tim 1:7). I claimed that promise in that moment. And when I did, the lie actually seems stupid and really obvious. Of course I can't do it all by myself! I wasn't ever meant to walk in my own power (or lack thereof). Whew! But, I can do all things THROUGH Christ, who strengthens me (Philippians 4:13). I can walk in the path he's laid out before me—empowered and emboldened by his Spirit. I can rest knowing God has given me everything I need to do what he's called me to do. This is just one real-life moment where Scripture in my head calmed my heart and assured me of the exact truth I needed to cling to.

This isn't just for me, it's for everyone.

When you memorize verses, those words get into your psyche. They start showing up in different situations, putting a lens over how you interpret things. Those words you've learned come to you when you'd least expect it, refocusing your mind. They give guidance and wisdom and life. In every situation, but especially in difficult ones, they ground you to the truth that transcends circumstance. At least for me, God has used memorizing Scripture as the biggest agent of good in my day-to-day life. It's how I hear Jesus speaking to me, all the time, in his own words. It's how I keep Jesus at the center of my heart. Let me tell you just a couple of the ways that "fixing his words" in my mind have changed my heart and therefore my ministry.

1. DAYS ARE LONG.
I NEED TO REFOCUS.

Even when I spend time in God's Word first thing in the morning, by the time I hit the pavement, I'm head-down, task-focused, just trying to tackle all the things I have coming at me. I need CONSTANT refocusing. I need a reminder to rest in God's goodness when I'm work-weary (Ps 116:7), to rely on his Spirit when I am doing things in my own strength (2 Tim 1:7), and to take "kindness detours" from my plan for my day (Eph. 4:32). These are just three verses I've memorized; and what an impact they've had on me! Instead of going my own way throughout my day, those words actually light up the path God has for me.

2. I AM NOT WISE. GOD IS.

We all want to believe that we have these disarming nuggets of truth to drop on people, the perfect words for every situation. The truth is, we just don't. At least I don't! If I'm being honest, ANYTHING I ever say—anything of any value, anything wise or good or true, anything at all—didn't originate with me! I totally lifted it from the Bible. Praise God though; he loves when we plagiarize him! He wants us to know his words and share them. And when we have his words on the tip of our tongues, we've got the best, right words for every situation.

3. GOD'S WORD IS LIFE.

Jesus gives us a great illustration to help us understand the life-giving nature of spending time with him in his Word. He tells us in John 15 that we are branches and he's the vine. Just like branches must remain attached to the vine to live, we too cannot live without staying connected to the life-giving source: Jesus. In verse 7, he tells us the way we abide in him is by *keeping his words in us*. They are HOW we stay connected to him and know him. Now, this doesn't mean if we don't memorize Scripture, we can't be connected to him. Surely, we can be in his Word in other ways. But one really great way to have his words in us is by memorizing them. It's a constant connection wherever we are, all day (and night) long.

4. LIFE ISN'T ALL RAINBOWS AND PUPPY DOGS.

All of us have very real struggles in this imperfect world. We deal with loss and hardship, relational difficulties, work strife, failures, and worry. When we memorize God's Word, we have it with us, on-the-ready for whatever life might throw at us. There have been specific times in my own life when particular words from God through Scripture were my lifeline. I look back on those times through the lens of the way God used those sweet verses to pull me through.

When Jesus's words are the center of our minds and hearts, they have the power to transform us into people who don't just know about him, but who truly *know* him.

5. YOUR STORIES ARE POWERFUL.

As God uses the Scripture in your own life, be sure to share those stories with the kids in your ministry. Let them see that you are relying on the Lord and His Word as you go through your day. Let them know that you are memorizing Scripture just like you are encouraging them to. Your stories carry power. Don't keep them to yourself.

Memorizing Bible verses might sound like a stretch to you.

You might be thinking, "Sure, this all sounds amazing. But, my brain? NO WAY! I don't even remember basic math!" I'm right there with you. I'm no great brain talent. But, I've got a crazy-simple method that anyone can use to memorize Scripture. Here's how it works:

- Find a verse that you want to remember.
- On one side of a notecard, write out the verse.
- On the reverse side, write out the first letter of each word in the verse.
- Now here comes the crazy part. Your mind WANTS to remember what those letters stand for. Every time you see those letters, you're prompted to remember the words they represent.
- Quiz yourself until you remember the verse.

You can do this! You can memorize God's words. So, here's my challenge for you: the next time you open your Bible, find a verse that speaks to your heart and memorize it. Those words will bring you life and power and peace. They'll come to your mind when you need them or come out of your mouth when someone else does. When you memorize and meditate on Scripture it tethers you to Jesus. Try it out with just one small verse and see what God will do. Then do the same thing with the kids in your ministry. That head knowledge will become heart knowledge which makes all the difference in the world.

Memorizing Scripture centers our hearts on Jesus. [period]

| LIVING IT OUT |

- *Stop and evaluate. Are you spending more time doing Jesus-y things than you're spending with Jesus?*

- *Are you leading your ministry by example, keeping Jesus at the center of your heart?*

- *What areas of your life or ministry do you need to find and memorize verses for?*

JESUS TO LITTLES
PRESCHOOL
Josh Zello

> Whoever welcomes one of these little children in my name welcomes me; and whoever welcomes me does not welcome me but the one who sent me.
> -Mark 9:37

Think of the front row seat to the amazing gospel ministry the disciples had. First, they saw Jesus turn water into wine at a wedding feast in John 2. Their response to this made sense. When Jesus *"revealed His glory... His disciples believed in Him"* (John 2:11). They stood in awe as Jesus gave sight to the blind, filled nets with fish in broad daylight, healed the crippled, fed a crowd of 5,000 with one little boy's lunchbox, raised a man from the dead, walked on water, and told a storm to be quiet. On top of all of that, they saw Jesus himself be transfigured on a mountain, showing them that the glory of the Lord was upon him. All of this would have humbled most of us. All of this would have made most of us feel small as we stood in awe of the majesty, splendor, and greatness of Jesus. Instead, Jesus' disciples began to argue about which of them was the greatest! In Mark 9, Jesus confronts this with an object illustration. We all know how effective object illustrations can be. This one was so effective that we're still talking about it today. Jesus held a child in his arms. The Bible uses the word for infant or toddler. This was the smallest of children. This was a preschooler. Remember, in Biblical society, children weren't held in high esteem. The world wasn't friendly towards children. Unlike today, where some might consider it to be better for children to be seen and not heard, children weren't to be seen or heard. Children were seen as no better than slaves. They weren't worth spending time thinking about, let alone serving. The writers of Table Talk Magazine put it like this: *"Children—and women for that matter— were not viewed as having much worth. Like servants, any value they had was in connection to the head of the household. They were seen as having little intrinsic worth."* Even today, the world looks over or through children, not at children. The world wants to rush them past childhood and into adulthood - forming them into "productive members of society." But Jesus turned this thought upside down with one sentence: *"Whoever receives one child like this in My name receives Me; and whoever receives Me does not receive Me, but Him who sent Me"* (Mark 9:37).

Think of the great honor of the child held in Jesus' hands. Maybe one day, by the grace of God, this child was able to grow up and look back at this moment to her own children and say "Jesus used me as an object lesson! Jesus pointed to me, held me, loved me, and welcomed me." Jesus prioritizes children. He has time for them. He has time for their curiosity. He has time for their endless questions. He has time for their temper tantrums. He has time for their insistence of the same book being read seven times. Not only does Jesus have time for preschoolers, but he cherishes them. They're precious to him. He enjoys them. He loves their laughter, their songs, and their constant learning. He wants to hear their prayers. He wants to spend time with them, and to empower them to serve his Father. Jesus formed them in his image for them to know and to glorify him, and He's the first to welcome them in his own name.

To be great preschool ministers, we're called to receive children in Jesus' name. We're called to welcome children in Jesus' name. When we welcome children in Jesus' name, we welcome Jesus himself. When we welcome Jesus, we welcome the Father. To be truly great is to serve the least of these, and Jesus specified that serving children is a perfect demonstration of this. "Jesus used word and deed to teach us about children… In welcoming them, He said 'we welcome not just Jesus but the God who sent him'. Children, Jesus taught, are among the most cherished of God's cherished," said Nove Vailaau. In this moment, Jesus demonstrated to his disciples how to welcome children. Jesus demonstrated what it looked like to be great by serving the least of these, the most vulnerable.

Preschoolers can't sustain themselves. They don't know how to cook for themselves, and it's even a bad idea for them to eat without adult supervision. They need help taking baths and getting dressed. They don't have emotional regulation skills, and cry over anything and everything. They don't earn money, or contribute to society in ways often most valued. Instead, they're needy and high maintenance. They're messy, and somehow sticky all the time. But Jesus loves them abundantly and calls us to serve them faithfully! "There is no political payback in serving children: they can't vote. And they don't give speeches about how great your helpfulness is," said Pastor John Piper upon reflecting on this very text. "In fact they pretty much take for granted that you will take care of them. They don't make a big deal out of the fact that you pour your life out for them. And so, children prove, more clearly than any other kind of people, whether you are truly great or not—whether you live to serve or live to be praised."

The first way I can think of that we welcome preschoolers in Jesus' name is by caring for their wellbeing. We've all heard it, and most of us have even said it: What we do is kid's ministry - not childcare. This statement comes with good intentions. As leaders in preschool ministry, we have a right desire for our churches to respect what we do as "real ministry." We worry that people see us as just diaper changers, snack dispensers, and puppet entertainers. We worry that what we spend so much time thinking through with gospel intentionality isn't seen as ministry, but instead, is seen as just "childcare." We worry that the church doesn't value the spiritual significance of the work that we do.

What you do is not *just* childcare, but a big part of it *is* childcare. See, effective church childcare is real ministry. When we care for the physical needs of children, we're showing them that we serve a God who cares about their physical needs (Matthew 6:26-27). When we care for the spiritual needs of children by prioritizing child discipleship, even on a preschool level, we're showing them that there's a God who cares about their souls and wants to spend eternity with them. The best way to introduce preschoolers to Jesus is to care for them well, physically and spiritually. This means that when we take the time to make sure that our first aid kits are fully stocked, we're welcoming preschoolers in Jesus' name. When we teach our volunteer teams CPR, we're welcoming preschoolers in Jesus' name. When we run and maintain background checks on our volunteers, we're welcoming preschoolers in Jesus' name. Ensuring that toys are safe matters. Making sure there's no choking hazards in the toddler room matters. Finding a clear way to communicate kids' allergies matters. Having fire safety and lockdown plans matter. See, even the most seemingly practical matters have spiritual significance. When preschoolers learn that church is a safe place for them, they will open their hearts readily to meet Jesus.

Providing a safe ministry to children and their families speaks well of the name of Jesus, showing families that we serve a God who cares for their wellbeing perfectly. Every meal our preschoolers enjoy is provided by Jesus, their Great Provider. The clothes on their backs and the shoes on their feet are gifts from the Creator and Sustainer. Jesus cares about the physical wellbeing of the children in our care, and He's the one who empowers us to do so, too. But not only does Jesus care for the physical wellbeing of these children, he perfectly cares for their spiritual wellbeing, too. Jesus is the one who came to live perfectly, love everybody always, then die on a cross, and rise again to bring them to the Father. Jesus takes care of every need of them, physically and spiritually. When we take care of the needs of children, we're showing them Jesus, and welcoming them in his name.

Another way that we do this is by caring about their joy. Joy is the language of children, and as a preschool minister, you need to learn to speak joy. May your children's ministry be filled with laughter and fun. Guide kids in what it means to find joy in him through purposeful and intentional play. Decorate your kid's church room to make it appealing and joy-filled. Even if that's just colorful walls, and signage at eye-level to children, create a space where preschoolers want to be!

Create a space where they can form fun, Christ-centered childhood memories. Model to them what it means to find joy in Jesus. Show them on your happy days what that looks like. Show them on your sad or difficult days what that looks like. Take care of your own heart, so that you can take care of theirs. Seek joy in the Lord for yourself, so that you can seek joy in the Lord for them. In John 15:10-12, Jesus tells his followers *"if you keep My commandments, you will remain in My love; just as I have kept My Father's commandments and remain in His love. These things I have spoken to you so that My joy may be in you, and that your joy may be made full."* Jesus wants our joy to be full, and He knows that this can only happen when we're abiding in him. Jesus cares about the joy of preschoolers. He takes delight in their laughter. He wants them to have ultimate joy in him, as they seek to obey his commandments and remain in his love. The most joyful place we can be is in Jesus, and that's just as true for our preschoolers. Now joy doesn't mean happiness every single moment. Joy sometimes includes momentary happiness, but not always. Think of Hebrews 12:2. *"...Jesus, the originator and perfecter of the faith, who for the joy set before Him endured the cross, despising the shame, and has sat down at the right hand of the throne of God."* It may be hard for you to imagine Jesus happily going to the cross. It was a painful, brutal experience. But it was a joyful one! Jesus knew what was coming next, and perfectly obeyed his Father's plan. Following after God is the desire of happiness; to reach God is happiness itself," said Saint Augustine.

The joy of the Lord was set before Jesus, giving him strength to endure the unimaginable. As we welcome preschoolers in Jesus' name by caring for their joy, we're teaching them to endure the suffering that will inevitably be part of their life story. Even preschoolers can begin to understand that on sad days, happy days, scary days, or confusing days… Jesus is good, and we can have joy in him.

We also welcome preschoolers in Jesus' name by caring for their righteousness. It's not loving to let children remain in their sin, and not to train them up in righteousness. Reflecting on discipline, Albert Barnes wrote, "It shall be a part of their future glory that they shall be all under divine instruction and guidance." Instruct your preschoolers in righteousness. Don't be afraid to gently call out their sin and to speak frankly about it. Disciple them by pointing them to Jesus and His perfect righteousness. The most practical way to care for the righteousness of our children is by consistently teaching them Scripture. In 2 Timothy 3:16-17, we read *"All Scripture is inspired by God and beneficial for teaching, for rebuke, for correction, for training in righteousness; so that the man or woman of God may be fully capable, equipped for every good work."* The most loving thing you can do every Sunday morning in children's ministry is to teach them from the Word of God! The way that preschoolers begin to truly know Jesus is by knowing His Word, and the way that they truly begin to know His Word is by getting in the Word. Have Bibles accessible every Sunday morning, and teach Biblical literacy. When you stand and teach, or even when you lead a small group circle time; hold the open Bible in your hands. This communicates to them that you're not just making it up as you go. What you're teaching is of the utmost importance because of where it's coming from and who it's pointing to.

Jesus perfectly cares for their righteousness, so much so that he actually stands ready to give them his perfect righteousness! Children come into this world as sinners who sin. They're born as sons of Adam, needing salvation. Then as soon as they're old enough to start to choose right and wrong, they're inclined to choose wrong. We don't have to teach children to sin. It comes naturally. Spend any amount of time in a preschool classroom and you'll see it firsthand. Children know how to lie, to steal, to hit, and how to direct their anger at other children. On the other hand, you can't just teach children how to be good. If you spend all of your time teaching moralistic values, you'll end up with kids trying to earn salvation and failing at it. Or, you'll get boastful kids that think they're good enough to earn entry to the Father's throne room on their own. So what do we do? We point them to the righteousness of Christ! Jesus was born outside of the curse of Adam. Jesus was not born as a sinner who sins. Jesus wasn't inclined towards doing what was wrong, but instead, perfectly obeyed his Father each and every day. Jesus did all of his chores when he was asked, never lied to his parents, never stole anything, and never had to repent for unrighteous anger. In one of the greatest miracles in world history, Jesus lived as a man, but did it perfectly- without sin. Jesus' perfect life isn't a model for us to point to kids for them to imitate. Instead, with his death and resurrection, Jesus provided a way for the kids in our ministries to put on his righteousness. Think of it like a coat. Jesus allows us to put on his perfect righteousness by having faith in him. The kids we serve have access to this righteousness, and we welcome them in Jesus' name when we show them how!

Let's go back to Mark 9. Jesus doesn't scold his disciples for wanting to be great. Instead, he redefines for them what it means to be great. It's not a sinful thing for you to want to be a great children's minister. I want you to be a great children's minister! But we need to make sure that our definition of greatness is a Biblical one. To be great is to be received by the Father. To be received by the Father is to be received by Jesus. To be received by Jesus is to receive the least of these in His name. To receive the least of these in his name is to receive children. Receive the children. Welcome them in Jesus' name! Care for their wellbeing. Take care of their physical needs - and point them to Jesus by providing them with full bellies and clean diapers. Care for their spiritual needs. Point them to the one true God with everything that's within you. Care for their joy! Teach them to abide in the Lord Jesus and to obey his commandments. Laugh with them. Play with them. Create Christ-centered childhood memories. And lastly, care for their righteousness. Teach them to read and cherish the Bible, because that's where righteousness is found as they begin to see, to know, and to love Jesus for who he is and what he's done.

In Matthew 19, Jesus was teaching a large group. As he taught, he was challenged with tough questions on the theology of marriage and remarriage. This was important stuff! The Pharisees leaned in as they attempted to find fault with what Jesus said, and the disciples were armed with questions of their own. Suddenly, in what must have felt like an interruption, children were brought to Jesus. In all of the paintings we've seen of this moment, we see quiet and angelic-looking full grown children sitting at Jesus' feet and on his lap. But in the original text, the word here for children is again the same word for infants. These are really young children. When the disciples step in between Jesus and these littles as they attempt to protect Jesus and his important work, Jesus stops and rebukes them. These children are a very big part of the important work Jesus had come to do. He welcomed them, caring for their wellbeing, their joy, and their righteousness.

I pray you grow in welcoming preschoolers in Jesus' name. May the children who walk into your ministry this Sunday feel welcomed... not in your church's name. Not in your name. Not in their own name, but in Jesus' name. "You serve a child best when you receive a child and care for a child and spend time with a child and hold a child NOT in the name of the child, or in the name of mankind or in the name of mercy or in the name of America's future, but in the name of Jesus, the Son of the living God," said John Piper. We're not called to simply welcome children, but to do so in his name. The name of Jesus matters.

There's only one way to greatness. There's only one way for you to be the best children's ministry leader you can be, and for your children's ministry to be the best it can be. There's only one way for children to be cared for physically and spiritually, filled with joy, and covered with perfect righteousness... Jesus. [period]

[LIVING IT OUT]

- *How does the world see children? How does your local church see children?*

- *What does it mean to welcome children in Jesus' name?*

- *Why do children need the righteousness of Christ? How do they obtain it?*

JESUS. [HEART]
WORSHIP

Jason Houser

[
Therefore, I urge you, brothers and sisters, in view of God's
mercy, to offer your bodies as a living sacrifice, holy and
pleasing to God—this is your true and proper worship.
-Romans 12:1
]

Take a deep breath before you read this chapter. Pause and
pray... asking the Spirit to help you understand how you can use this
encouragement to teach the young people the Lord has placed in your
care.

Close your eyes. Engage your imagination and look around the
room where your children are led in worship. Look at their beautiful
faces. Consider how deeply you love each one of these kids - and how
you have experienced the unexplainable joy in their victories and the

heartfelt pain of their struggles as you've walked with them (and their families) through the different seasons.

I am seeing a young girl's face in our children's ministry named Jessica. Her parents had two older children when she was born. They thought their family was complete, but God had a wonderful surprise for them. I prayed with Jessica's parents at her baby dedication service. She became a part of our elementary children's church when she was 5 years old and I'll tell you this, the girl loves to worship Jesus. She has the sweetest smile and a joy that is incredibly infectious. When she was 7 years old, she asked if she could help lead the hand motions for our scripture worship songs and I gladly invited her to lead worship with me.

This year, as a 9-year-old, she asked to be baptized. I sat in the congregation with tears in my eyes as our pastor read her testimony to the church about how she loved Jesus and wanted to let everyone know she was going to follow Him for her whole life. I believe Jessica is a child after God's heart. I am confident that her child-like faith will mature and she will continue to live as a follower and worshiper of God.

What is the name of a child in your ministry whom you have seen the Spirit of God working in their heart? Be encouraged to know that your own calling to serve in ministry to children and families is worth every challenge you face. These children and parents need us to come alongside them as they face the influence of a culture which I believe is unique to any other time in the history of the world. We can easily become overwhelmed and discouraged as we watch families break apart and kids shouldering the heavy burdens put on them by the world and the ever-confusing narratives that are being projected in media and culture. I believe we can make an eternal difference in each of these young lives by teaching them that God's Word is true and it is knowing and loving Him that will truly satisfy them. He created them to worship - and their joy will come when they love God and look to Him to define who they are and what truly matters most in life.

So, my desire for our time together is to help us consider how we can create an atmosphere of worship in our children's ministries. Worship that will impact these children so much that they take it into their homes, schools and ultimately into their adult lives. My hope is that our worship through music will overflow into a daily expression of a life of worship.

King David is famously known as a man after God's own heart and is credited with writing nearly half of the 150 Psalms in the Bible. Let's look at several of David's Psalms and process how we can help cultivate an environment to inspire a generation of young people with hearts that understand and express gratitude, joy, and praise in worship.

My heart is steadfast, God, my heart is steadfast;
I will sing, yes, I will sing praises!
Awake, my glory!
Awake, harp and lyre!
I will awaken the dawn.
I will praise You, Lord, among the peoples;
I will sing praise to you among the nations.
For Your goodness is great to the heavens
And your truth to the clouds.
Be exalted above the heavens, God;
May Your glory be above all the earth. - Psalm 57:7-11 (NASB)

I often hear people struggling to define the word "worship". I hear many definitions that are incomplete and the word worship itself is often used to describe services, or songs, or musical styles. I have discovered a new definition this year that I believe begins to help us get our arms around what it truly means to worship.

"Worship is when everything we are responds to everything God is."

YES! Listen to David's song from Psalm 57. He is confident in God's character...he is responding to everything God is. He says, "no wonder I can sing your praises." As if to say, "why in the world would you not desire to praise a God this great!" So in response, he calls his heart and his instruments to wake up and begin the day with thankful worship. He commits to singing God's praise among all the nations which God has made. And again, acknowledging the awesomeness of God, he creatively expresses the power of God's love and the expanse of his faithfulness. He lifts God's name and prays for his glory to shine over the earth.

So, how do we awaken this desire in the hearts of children like David prayed for here in his song? I believe we do this by creating an environment of praise through prayer and communication to children at their age level. It is also beneficial to use whatever creative tools you have available to engage the children in singing, praying to God, and worshiping Him.

Here's a simple outline of how I lead a worship time for children:

Pray: I begin every worship session with prayer, asking God to be present in our praise and to help us to focus our attention on Him.

Read: It is excellent to have a children's call to worship by reading a Psalm at the outset of the worship time. Psalm 100 is an incredible place to start. (I discuss this in further detail later).

Sing: Because I have been writing and recording scripture music for many years, I have a passion for teaching children God's Word. So, we begin our worship singing God's Word with joyful, upbeat scripture songs with hand motions. There are many great resources available to equip kids to sing the Word. I encourage you to include them in your worship time for children. There is power in singing God's Word and I see kids engage in a special way as they sing the Bible. At the same time that they are worshiping, we are helping kids get God's Word hidden in their hearts, just as it says in Psalm 119:9-11:

> *"How can a young man keep his way pure?*
> *By keeping it according to Your word.*
> *With all my heart I have sought You;*
> *Do not let me wander from Your commandments.*
> *I have treasured Your word in my heart,*
> *So that I may not sin against You."*

During the second half of our worship time, we typically sing vertical worship songs. We begin our sessions singing God's Word and then transition to singing directly to God. I briefly introduce each song and talk about the words we are singing and what they mean. Whether we are singing scripture songs or vertical worship songs, I believe it is important for all worshipers to process what they are singing, and communicating about, to their Creator. I am always careful to unpack words that may be outside the vocabulary of my young worshipers... asking questions and processing through the lyrics with them.

Pray: As we finish our worship time, I typically pray out of the last song and pray a prayer that is connected to our worship time. For example, if we are singing about God's Word, I will thank God for His Word and tell Him we trust Him and believe His Word is truth. I will ask Him to teach us in our class time through His Word and to help us to know Him and love Him more through what we learn.

This simple outline is merely a framework to equip the worship leader to engage with the kids and lead them to worship. Psalm 57 outlines the greater heart behind the worship: to inspire young hearts to acknowledge and respond to the greatness of who God truly is. Kids will resonate with the word pictures that David expressed when he wrote "God's love is as high as the heavens and His faithfulness reaches to the clouds". These are powerful Biblical images for worship leaders to express to their kids. It is good to give the children an opportunity to share what they believe these pictures represent. This will help give them an understanding of God so they can respond to him from their hearts.

> *The one thing I ask of the Lord-the one thing I seek the most-is to live in the house of the Lord all the days of my life, delighting in the Lord's perfections and meditating in His temple. At his sanctuary I will offer sacrifices with shouts of joy, singing and praising the Lord with music. -Psalm 27:4 & 6 (NLT)*

> *One thing I have asked of the Lord, that I shall seek;*
> *That I may dwell in the house of the Lord all the days of my life,*
> *To behold the beauty of the Lord and to meditate in his temple.*
> *-Psalm 27:4 & 6 (NASB)*

I believe this song of David is an incredible illustration of the posture of worship. It demonstrates what it looks like to be a person diligently seeking after the heart of God. David focuses his energy and attention on God. He tells Him that He alone is the "one thing" that David wants most in his life. His desire is to worship God by delighting in His perfection and deeply considering who He is and all that He has done. He does this by joyfully offering "shouts of joy singing and praising the Lord with music."

In our children's ministry, we want to show children an example of what this looks like in corporate worship. David expressed his affections for the Lord with his energetic musical offering of gratitude and praise, and lifting up the name of the Lord.

Psalm 100 also provides another excellent picture of what this kind of worship looks like:

Shout for joy to the Lord all the earth. Worship the Lord with gladness. Come before Him with joyful songs, know that the Lord is God. It is he who made us and we are his. We are his people the sheep of his pasture. Enter his gates with thanksgiving and his courts with praise; give thanks him and praise his name. For the Lord is good and his love endures forever; his faithfulness continues through all generations. Psalm 100 (NLT)

Shout joyfully to the Lord, all the earth.
Serve the Lord with jubilation;
Come before Him with rejoicing.
Know that the Lord, Himself is God;
It is He who made us, and not we ourselves;
We are His people and the sheep of His pasture.
Enter His gates with thanksgiving,
And His courts with praise.
Give thanks to Him, bless His name.
For the Lord is good;
His mercy is everlasting
And His faithfulness is to all generations. -Psalm 100 (NASB)

The whole earth is called to bring shouts of joy and glad worship to the Lord. Again, we see how David is worshiping God with all He is as a response to all God is. He affirms his confidence again that He knows the Lord is God - that He is the One who created us and we belong to Him."

Our worshipful response should be to come into His presence thanking Him and moving closer to him as we praise Him. And what does David praise him for next? He praises Him for his goodness, his eternal love, and his faithfulness to every generation.

It is great to engage kids in thanks before you sing a song of gratefulness to the Lord. Ask children to share what they're thankful to God for. Go around the room and give them ample time to express what they are thankful for from the Lord. Encourage them to give God the praise and the credit for every good thing in their lives. Then ask them to share something that is true about who God is, about His character. Psalm 100 is definitely one of my favorite go-to scriptures to share with kids and other worship leaders. It is the scripture I read aloud at the outset of the worship times to share with kids how the Bible instructs us to worship the Lord.

> *O Lord, hear me as I pray; pay attention to my groaning. Listen to my cry for help, my King and my God, for I pray to no one but you. Listen to my voice in the morning, Lord. Each morning I bring my requests to you and wait expectantly.*
>
> *But let all who take refuge in you rejoice; let them ever sing for joyful praises forever. Spread your protection over them, that all who love your name be filled with joy. - Psalm 5:1-3, 11 (NLT)*
>
> *Listen to my words, Lord,*
> *Consider my sighing.*
> *Listen to the sound of my cry for help, my King and my God.*
> *For to You I pray.*
> *In the morning, Lord, You will hear my voice;*
> *In the morning I will present my prayer to You and be on watch.*
> *But rejoice, all who take refuge in You,*
> *Sing for joy forever!*
> *And may You shelter them,*
> *That those who love Your name may rejoice in You.*
> *-Psalm 5:1-3, 11 (NASB)*

For us as children's ministry leaders and for our children's worship leaders, there is nothing more important than staying connected to the source of our worship. In John 15, Jesus tells us how critical it is for us to remain in Him if we are going to have a fruitful life for God's Kingdom. Jesus illustrates what it looks like for us to abide in Him. John 15:5 says,

"I am the vine, you are the branches; the one who remains in Me, and I in him bears much fruit, for apart from Me you can do nothing (NASB)."

If we desire to create an atmosphere of worship for our children, we need to be spending time with Jesus in the secret place and abiding in him, for nothing of Kingdom value is possible outside of Him. The passage goes on to encourage us in John 15:11 that when we do abide in Him, we will have a fruitful life and His joy will be in us, *"These things I have spoken to you so that My joy may be in you, and that your joy may be made full."*

The picture I love to use connected with this passage as it relates to worship is this. When we abide is Christ, we are His chosen instruments used for our greatest purpose: to be fruit, or in other words, to bring spiritual nourishment and life to others and ultimately glory to God. As we are being used by the Lord as His instruments, we are resonating with joy in the same way a physical instrument resonates and comes to life in the hands of a master musician. We are being used for our created purpose and God's song for our life, the beautiful and unique melody he crafted for our story, is being played through God's greater story for us... and in those moments I believe we get to resonate with the fullness of His joy.

So, how do we practice abiding in Jesus in a way that will help us lead worship?

I recently started a simple practice that has a profound impact on my time with Jesus. I start my morning prayer and devotion time listening to at least one worship song. Sounds insanely simple and not at all profound, doesn't it? But don't underestimate the power of small habits compounded over time. Often one song turns into multiple worship songs as I pray and write in my journal. If you don't already have a subscription to a music streaming service, like Spotify, Apple Music, or Amazon; it is definitely worth $10 per month to have unlimited access to worship albums and playlists. It makes it effortless to begin this life-changing habit that will tune your heart to the Lord as you begin your day.

David sang Psalm 5 as a petition to God to hear his morning prayer. He seeks God in the morning and expectantly waits for God to answer. This Psalm concludes with David encouraging all who take refuge in God to be filled with joy and sing praise to him as a response.

Not sure where to start your own morning worship playlist? "Morning By Morning" by Pat Barrett is a great song to use as you launch into this new practice:

> Daily, daily, I surrender,
> Grace for today is all that I need,
> Surprised by your mercy that's new every morning
> Awaken my soul to sing,
> Awaken my soul to sing,
> I will trust where you lead,
> I will trust when I can't see
> Morning by morning,
> Great is your faithfulness to me

This is just one example of "oceans" of songs, excuse the pun, that can lead you into worship as you pursue God like David did at the outset of your day. This time with Jesus will prepare you and your team as a leader of children's worship. I believe the greatest way to make Jesus the center of our ministries is to make Him the center of our own lives.

When Jesus taught His disciples how to pray, He told them it was critical to spend time with the Lord in the "inner room" or the "secret place", as recorded in Matthew 6:6. He told them not to be like an actor that is performing on a stage to be seen and admired by people.

But you, when you pray, go into your inner room, close your door and pray to your Father who is in secret, and your Father who sees *what is done* in secret will reward you.

We prepare our hearts to lead children in worship by making it a priority to spend time alone with God. It is not to be done as a religious practice. It is the way to cultivate a heart of worship through spending time in relationship with Jesus. Take an inventory of your time and remove some lesser important things in your personal or ministry life in order to make sure you are spending time in the secret place.

Jesus. [period]

In order to awaken and engage young ones in worship and prepare your own heart in worship as a ministry leader, it all centers around our relationships. First and foremost, our relationship with God and our personal life of worship. Then our love for the Lord will naturally flow into our corporate worship and our leadership. The leaders, after seeking after God's heart, will be able to teach and inspire your hearts to worship Jesus. [period]

[LIVING IT OUT]

- *How do we awaken the hearts of children by using gathering times together as a church to inspire them to live their lives as worshipers of Jesus every day?*

- *How do we engage young people in worship and demonstrate what it looks like to be a child after God's heart.*

- *How can we as leaders most effectively prepare to lead children in joy-filled, life-giving worship?*

JESUS FOR EVERY GENERATION
DISCIPLING TODAY'S KIDS

Brian Dembowczyk

> Hear, O Israel: The Lord our God, the Lord is one.
> Love the Lord your God with all your heart and
> with all your soul and with all your strength.
> These commandments that I give you today are to be
> on your hearts. Impress them on your children. Talk about
> them when you sit at home and when you walk along the
> road, when you lie down and when you get up.
> Tie them as symbols on your hands and bind them
> on your foreheads. Write them on the doorframes of your
> houses and on your gates.
> -Deuteronomy 6:4-9

Every generation has its fads. The 1960's tie-dyed everything it could get its hands on while gazing intently at lava lamps. The 1970's strutted around with its feathered hair and bellbottoms. The 1980's wore Swatch watches while trying to solve the Rubik's Cube. The 1990's collected Beanie Babies while listening to boy bands. The 2000's traded Pokémon cards on its way to flash mobs. And the 2010's played with fidget spinners when it wasn't doing the mannequin challenge.

It's kind of funny to think back on these fads now, especially the ones that we got caught up in. We remember the spell we were under; we simply had to have that toy or piece of clothing. It felt like the most important thing in the world because everyone who was anyone had it or wore it. We didn't want to miss out. But then, in the blink of an eye, it was over. We had all moved on to a new fad that would be all the rage for a few months. Then the process would repeat.

There isn't anything necessarily wrong with taking part in fads, but they do reveal something important about our fallen human nature: we are never satisfied. We are always chasing after the next best thing, thinking *it* will make us somebody and be what finally makes us happy.

We might not like to admit it, but we can easily follow fads in our churches and ministries, too. From various programs and events, to routines and schedules. And even to philosophies and resources; we can chase after the next "best" thing that makes our churches and ministries thrive and grow. For the most part, there isn't anything wrong with innovation. God created us to be creative like He is. Furthermore, our ministry context changes over time, making innovation something we should pursue rather than merely tolerate. But, we must be careful not to lose sight of the essential truth that while the *process* of ministry might change, the *goal* of ministry never should. From creation (and even before), God's intention has been that we live as image-bearers reflecting who He is to everyone and everything around us (Gen. 1:26–28). Sin marred our ability to do this, but Jesus, the perfect image of God (Col. 1:15; Heb. 1:3), came so that we might be forgiven and able to fulfill our created purpose once more. What is the unchanging goal of kids ministry, then? It is to make our kids disciple-making disciples who (1) know and believe in Jesus, (2) love Jesus, and (3) live like Jesus.

That last part is critical, but often overlooked. We are called "Christians" because we are to act like Him. The term literally means "little Christs."

Now, this doesn't mean we are to look *exactly* like Jesus. We don't have to wear robes and sandals, round up twelve guys (being sure one is a dud), and travel throughout modern day Israel, Palestine, and Syria teaching and performing miracles. In fact, we *shouldn't* try to do everything Jesus did. He is God, and we are not. But this does mean that we look at the human characteristics Jesus demonstrated in perfection, and in the power of the Holy Spirit, seek to pattern our lives after them. It means we seek to love like Jesus loved. To care for people like Jesus cared. To obey God like Jesus obeyed. To be humble like Jesus was humble. How we disciple kids to do this might change, but that we disciple kids to do this must never change.

MODERN CHALLENGES TO OUR ANCIENT CALLING

Can we admit that our calling as kidmin leaders isn't easy? It might *sound* easy, but it is far from easy to disciple kids to know Jesus, love Jesus, and look like Jesus. In many ways, it's becoming even more difficult because of our shifting culture. Take the relentless march of consumerism, for example.

Consumerism is the blight of our culture that declares material possessions give life meaning. "What you own will make you happy," consumerism has whispered for decades and now shouts into our kids' ears and hearts. The problem is two-fold. First, that consumerism *can* satisfy us is an outright lie. God, not the latest iPhone, is what our hearts ultimately long for. Material possessions aren't inherently evil, but they can often serve as a self-administered anesthesia to dull that God-given ache for Him. Second, that consumerism *wants* to satisfy us is an outright lie. Consumerism may be sinister, but it is also clever. It has created a state of our kids perpetually needing to need. It dangles the next material possession, such as an iPhone, before our kids with the promise that it is what they need; and if they only own it, they will finally be content. But consumerism doesn't want us to be content. It needs us to be discontent or else it goes out of business. It needs us to buy that "better" new iPhone a year from now. Consumerism isn't new to our generation of kids, but it seems to be cranking into overdrive to disciple our kids and shape them in its image as god. The same is true of social media.

At the beginning of 2022, Facebook had roughly 3 billion users, doubling that total from just five years before.[1] Worldwide, nine out of ten youth are believed to use social media each day.[2] Recent studies from the United States and Europe reveal that most eleven-year-olds own a smartphone, and eight- to twelve-year-olds use electronic devices for nearly five hours a day.[3] We might not like it, but the reality is that most of our kids are fully immersed in social media, which is discipling them in its own way. Social media has been proven to increase narcissism, which kids seem to be especially vulnerable to.[4] If consumerism is discipling our kids toward a false notion of happiness, social media is discipling them toward a false notion of identity. Social media allows us to shape an image of who we want to be for others to believe. Truth gives way to the currency of "likes" and comments that our kids have been told will make them someone who matters.

It shouldn't be surprising, then, that as our kids are being discipled by consumerism, social media, and other false gospels; they are less prone to recognize their need for the one true gospel of Jesus Christ. Riches in Christ give way to earthly riches. Identity in Christ gives

---

1 Vincent Henzel and Anders Håkansson, "Hooked on Virtual Social Life. Problematic Social Media Use and Associations with Mental Distress and Addictive Disorders," *PLoS ONE* 16, no. 4 (April 2021): 2; Julia Brailovskaia and Jürgen Margraf, "Comparing Facebook Users and Facebook Non-Users: Relationship between Personality Traits and Mental Health Variables—An Exploratory Study," *PloS One* 11, no. 12 (December 2016): 1.

2 Henzel and Håkansson, 2.

3 Ibid., 3.

4 Julia Brailovskaia and Jürgen Margraf, "Comparing Facebook Users and Facebook Non-Users: Relationship between Personality Traits and Mental Health Variables—An Exploratory Study," *PloS One* 11, 12 (December 2016): 11.

way to online identity. Hope found in Christ gives way to hope found in the world. We can feel this in our weary souls, but we can also see it in the data. Twenty-somethings are leaving the church in alarming numbers. Some studies indicate a drop-out rate of between 40% to 50%, while others show up to 70% or even 75%.[5] Not only do young adults attend church less often than in the past, but many also no longer even identify with the Christian faith. It is estimated that 20% to 30% of those who came of age in the 2000's do not identify with a religion, a significant increase from the 5% who came of age in the 1950's or before.[6] Undergirding this alarming data is another sobering statistic: 80% of college students who dropped out of church didn't intend to do so.[7] These young adults weren't in active rebellion against the church or the Christian faith; rather, they simply weren't well-grounded in the faith. They weren't hostile; they were merely disinterested.

The news gets worse when we look at what children, teens, and young adults believe:

- 64% of teens do not believe the Bible is accurate in all it teaches.[8]
- Most teens believe that Jesus may have sinned.[9]
- 42% do not believe that God is all-powerful, all-knowing Creator.[10]
- 81% do not believe they need to tell others about Christ.[11]
- 79% do not deny that good people can earn their way into heaven.[12]

---

5 "Reasons 18- to 22-Year-Olds Drop Out of Church," *Lifeway Research* (blog), August 7, 2007, https://lifewayresearch.com/2007/08/07/reasons-18-to-22-year-olds-drop-out-of-church/; Kathryn Lofton, "Religion and the Authority in American Parenting," *Journal of the American Academy of Religion* 84, no. 3 (September 2016): 828; Kara Powell and Chap Clark, *Sticky Faith: Everyday Ideas to Build Lasting Faith in Your Kids* (Grand Rapids, MI: Zondervan, 2011), 15, Kindle.

6 Ibid.

7 Powell and Clark, 16, Kindle.

8 George Barna, *Revolutionary Parenting: What the Research Shows Really Works* (Carol Stream, IL: Tyndale House Publishers, Inc., 2010), loc 307.

9 Ibid., loc 319.

10 Ibid., loc 324.

11 Ibid., loc 310.

12 Ibid., loc 316.

- 43% do not consider faith very important to them.[13]
- Fewer than 1 in 10 young adults lists faith as his or her top priority.[14]
- Only 3% of adults between 18 and 41 embrace a biblical worldview.[15]

In their landmark 2005 book *Soul Searching*, Christian Smith and Melinda Lundquist Denton found that teens who were raised in the faith are "incredibly inarticulate" about the Christian faith.[16] Most either don't understand or accept the core doctrines of Christian faith, preferring instead to live with "faith" operating in the "mental background of their lives."[17] Smith and Denton concluded that most teenagers see life through a lens they call "Moralistic Therapeutic Deism," which is marked by five core beliefs:

1. A God exists who created and orders the world and watches over human life on earth.
2. God wants people to be good, nice, and fair to each other, as taught in the Bible and by most world religions.
3. The central goal of life is to be happy and to feel good about oneself.
4. God does not need to be particularly involved in one's life except when God is needed to resolve a problem.
5. Good people go to heaven when they die.[18]

Furthermore, when young churchgoers were asked what words describe Christianity, 80% chose "antihomosexual," 52% chose

---

13 Ibid., loc 312.

14 David Kinnaman and Gabe Lyons, *Unchristian: What a New Generation Really Thinks about Christianity—and Why It Matters* (Grand Rapids, MI: Baker Books, 2007), 23.

15 Ibid., 75. The authors define a biblical worldview as believing that (1) Jesus lived a sinless life, (2) God is all-powerful and all-knowing Creator, (3) salvation is a gift, (4) Satan is real, (5) a Christian is responsible for evangelizing, (6) the Bible is accurate in all it teaches, (7) moral truth exists, and (8) the Bible defines truth.

16 Christian Smith and Melinda Lundquist Denton, *Soul Searching: The Religious and Spiritual Lives of American Teenagers* (New York, NY: Oxford University Press, 2005), 131.

17 Ibid., 134–37.

18 Ibid., 162–63.

"judgmental," and 47% chose "hypocritical."[19] Considering how our kids define the Christian faith and the church, we shouldn't be surprised when they don't make *that* faith and church a priority.

All of this shows that our ministries have become much more challenging, but also much more important. The church has always played a role in discipling kids, but now more than ever we need to step forward to fulfill our calling. How do we do that, though? New ministry fads won't be the answer. Instead, the best thing we can do is to look back at a 3,400-year-old text, praying that God stirs our hearts and minds anew to disciple our kids faithfully.

GOD'S DISCIPLESHIP TRIAD IN THE SHEMA

Deuteronomy 6:4–9, known as the Shema, which is the Hebrew word for "hear" that begins it, is one of the most important passages in the Old Testament. God gave these instructions through Moses to the second generation of Hebrews after the Exodus as they prepared to enter the Promised Land. These six verses are packed with principles affirming our three-fold discipleship purpose.

> *Hear, Israel! The Lord is our God, the Lord is one! And you shall love the Lord your God with all your heart and with all your soul and with all your strength. These words, which I am commanding you today, shall be on your heart. -Deut. 6:4–6*

Three verses into the Shema, notice the focus is squarely on the discipler with no reference to the kids being discipled. This is critically important as it reminds us that before we can even think about discipling kids, we need to consider our own relationship with Christ. Do you

---

19 Kinnaman and Lyons, *Unchristian*, 33.

want to know where the battle for discipling our kids might just be won or lost? Right here with us.

Common sense tells us that we cannot give away something we don't have. As much as I would love to loan you a Ferrari, alas, I cannot because I don't own a Ferrari. (Now, if you need to borrow a slightly beat-up Toyota Corolla, we might be able to work something out.) How much more is this true with discipling kids? We have no hope of making disciple-making disciples who know Jesus, love Jesus, and live like Jesus if we are not disciple-making disciples who know Jesus, love Jesus, and live like Jesus. These verses remind us how to be that. We are to know doctrine rightly (v. 4), love Christ fully (v. 5), and rehearse the gospel repeatedly (v. 6). Or, put another way, we are to be disciples who follow Christ with our total being: our head, our heart, and our hands. Or put still another way, we are to be men and women whose orthodoxy (right doctrine) sparks orthopathy (right feelings), which in turn leads to orthopraxy (right conduct). We need to be followers of Jesus who are driven by this triad of knowledge, emotion, and practice if we want to disciple our kids to be the same.

> *And you shall repeat them diligently to your sons and speak of them when you sit in your house, when you walk on the road, when you lie down, and when you get up. -Deut. 6:7*

As the Shema pivots to focus on how discipleship occurs, we cannot miss the core audience of this message: parents. While the passage doesn't expressly state it is directed toward parents, who else would be able to fulfill the imperatives of this verse? The context is clearly one of everyday living—when you sit in the house (not in the church building), when you walk on the road (not down the church halls), when you lie down (in bed at home, not on a pew), and when you get up (out of bed, not from the pew when the pastor bellows). God's plan has always been for parents to be the primary disciplers of their children. It was parents who were to teach their children of the Passover and God's deliverance of His people from Egypt (Ex. 12:26–27; 13:14). It was parents who were to tell their children about the Jordan River crossing (Josh. 4:21–22). It is parents who are to instruct their children in the Lord (Eph. 6:4). Why? Because while there might be greater theologians outside of the home and while others may have better training in how to teach a child, no one can have a greater degree of proximity and love for a child than a parent. Israel's priests could have told a firstborn son how he was spared from the death angel by the blood of a lamb, but for them it would have been secondhand and academic. A parent, however, telling his or her firstborn son would have been firsthand and emotional. God knew exactly what He was doing when He gave parents this task of discipleship.

This doesn't mean, of course, that we don't have an important role, too. It just means that we always need to remember we are secondary. So, we seek ways we can encourage and equip parents. We become their greatest advocates and cheerleaders. And we support their teaching in the home by what we teach in the church. But we also recognize that not every parent will fulfill this calling. Right or wrong, for better or worse, we may have to be the primary discipler for some of our kids. Therefore, we gladly step into that void and do the best we can for those children, as we also do all we can to see those parents step up so we can step back.

> *You shall also tie them as a sign to your hand, and they shall be as frontlets on your forehead. -Deut. 6:8*

As we drive down the final stretch of the Shema, we are reminded of the ultimate goal of discipleship—living differently. Some of the ancient Hebrews and orthodox Jews today take this verse literally and place portions of Scripture written on tiny scrolls inside small boxes called phylacteries and mezuzot, which are then strapped to the hand and forehead. While we can appreciate this dedication, God more than likely intended these instructions to be figurative. We do things with our hands. We see things with our eyes and think about them with our brains. This seems to be God's way of telling us that His Word is to guide us in all we do. It really takes us full circle back to verse 5. We are disciples who are driven by the head-heart-hands triad training kids to be disciples driven by the head-heart-hands triad. What our kids know and love matters. We surely want them to know and love Jesus. But we must not stop there. What they *do* matters just as much. We must reach this third aspect of discipleship. Don't take my word for it; take Jesus' word.

THE DISCIPLESHIP TRIAD THROUGHOUT SCRIPTURE

In Matthew 25:31–46 Jesus told the Parable of the Sheep and the Goats. This parable is set on the day of judgment, when believers (sheep) and unbelievers (goats) are separated for eternity. The sheep will enter the eternal kingdom (v. 34) while the goats will enter eternal punishment (v. 46). How is it that the sheep will be separated from the goats? By what they *did*:

> For I was hungry, and you gave Me something to eat; I was thirsty, and you gave Me something to drink; I was a stranger, and you invited Me in; naked, and you clothed Me; I was sick, and you visited Me; I was in prison, and you came to Me.
> -Matt. 25:35–36

Conversely, the goats will be identified by their failure to do these things (vv. 42–43). It's striking that Jesus doesn't say that the sheep will be recognized by a profession of faith they made. Or because they were baptized. Or because they attended church. Instead, they will be recognized by caring for other people. What's going on here?

Jesus isn't saying that the sheep *became* sheep by doing these things. Look at verse 33. The sheep were sheep to start with. What He is saying here is that true sheep will act like sheep. They can't help not to. Loving God and loving other people, the two greatest commandments (Matt.

22:36–40), do not make us disciples. Rather they reveal that we *are* disciples. Basically, Jesus reminds us that to be His disciple requires that we be fully His disciple—what we know and believe, what we love, and what we do. True disciples, then, must bear fruit (Matt. 7:15–20).

All Scripture is inspired by God and profitable, of course. However, if we had to choose four passages to be on our "Mount Rushmore" of Bible verses, Ephesians 2:1–9 would likely make many of our lists. It is perhaps the most beautiful expressions of salvation by grace anchored on those two amazing words in verse 4: "but God." The problem is the thought doesn't end in verse 9, but the one after:

> *For we are His workmanship, created in Christ Jesus for good works, which God prepared beforehand so that we would walk in them. -Eph. 2:10*

The word "for" connects all that came before this in a cause-and-effect relationship. Verses 1–9 is the cause. Verse 10 is the effect. Salvation by grace through faith is the cause. Doing good works is the effect. This is what the gospel is about in its fullness. We are surely to be *believers*, but true believers are to be *doers*. Or as James put it: "faith without works is dead" (James 2:26). Too many of our ministries are one or two-dimensional, focusing completely on belief and perhaps love. But as we have seen, we must include that third dimension of conduct. Our discipleship must be driven by this entire gospel triad of orthodoxy, orthopathy, and orthopraxy.

STEPS FOR DEVELOPING A DISCIPLESHIP TRIAD-DRIVEN MINISTRY

So, are you with me? Do you see how today's kids desperately need us to step up and disciple them in the way of Jesus so they know Jesus, love Jesus, *and* live like Jesus? I hope so. As we close here, let's consider five actions we can take to either retool our ministries to be driven by this triad or strengthen them if they already are.

Action 1: Take Personal Inventory

How are you doing spiritually? Really. How are you? Serving God can sometimes drain us and even drive us away from God. This is not because we are rebelling *against* Him, but because we fail to spend time *with* Him. We can focus so much on others, we fail to focus on ourselves. Therefore, it is important to take a frequent inventory of our spiritual health and do what we need to protect ourselves. The same is true of our leaders. Do you need to strengthen the consistency or quality of your times with the Lord? Try a different time of the day or place. Read a different Bible translation. Read through a Christian classic. Be creative and find how to energize your devotional times. Or perhaps you need to take a break. Even a one-day sabbatical can make a world of difference. Remember, you cannot give what you do not have and if you are running on fumes, you can be busy in ministry, but likely not effective. One of the best gifts you can give to your kids is the example of a disciple who loves Jesus and is living like Him.

Action 2: Clarify Your Discipleship Process

We know that in kids ministry, we aren't providing childcare or entertaining kids; we are discipling. But that doesn't happen by accident. We need to be intentional. Just like we need to enter our destination in a navigation app before we put our car into drive, we need to have our goal of discipleship and the process of how we will get there in mind. We need to cast this discipleship vision of teaching the gospel to our kids so their affections for Christ are stirred and they live like Him to our leaders and parents. Strive to reach the point that as you share it, they interrupt and finish it while rolling their eyes because they have heard it so much. When that happens, you know it's *beginning* to gel.

Action 3: Analyze Your Resources

Everything we do should support our ministry purpose. If it doesn't, why do it? So put everything under the microscope: curriculum, teachings, activities and events, everything. Do they support your ministry purpose? Do they teach the gospel clearly, help children love Christ more, and provide ways they can live their faith? If not, consider how you can adjust them so they do, or perhaps consider if you need to make any changes. Your goal here should be to rattle off an immediate answer of how every single resource advances your ministry's triad purpose.

Action 4: Partner with Your Parents

As the Shema reminds us, parents are our kids' primary disciplers. What ways can you encourage them more? How can you lift their spirits and give them life to fulfill their mission in the home, rather than dampen their spirits and steal life? How can you train and equip them? Perhaps you can partner with your lead pastor, or discipleship pastor if you have one, and develop workshops, clinics, retreats, or Bible studies on family discipleship. Will this take time and energy? Without a doubt it will. But every minute of time and every ounce of energy you invest in parents will have exponential power to affect your kids for Christ. If you only gave me one hour to minister to your kids, I would spend the first forty-five minutes with their parents, the next ten minutes with the ministry leaders, and the final five minutes with them.

Action 5: Do Less to Do More

Some of us are so focused on what happens on our campuses, we forget that more of life is spent off-campus. Let's be clear: gathering as believers is important and we all should want to do that. But that is not our ultimate goal on earth. We are to live *every* hour of *every* day in *every* place doing *everything* for God's glory (1 Cor. 10:31). That means on the one hand, we are to enjoy God's good gifts to us as an act of worship. That means on the other hand, we are to bear His image before a watching world so that we can be used by Him to draw others to Christ. This is why living like Jesus matters so much. We need, then, to be sure to give our kids and their families space to do just that.

This is what is in mind in the final verse of the Shema that we glossed over earlier:

> *You shall also write them on the doorposts of your house and on your gates. -Deut. 6:9*

The idea of the preceding verse is that God's Word, or the gospel is to shape us. Here we see that it is to identify us. In a way, we shouldn't have to tell others we are believers because our lives should show it. Remember, sheep live as sheep and goats can tell the difference. But those goats cannot tell a difference if the sheep are always hanging out together in the sheep pen. We need to put our lives on display, in humility, before a watching world so that they see the transforming power of the gospel as they hear the gospel professed by us, too (see 1 Cor. 4:9). We shouldn't pit the church against the community in the minds and hearts of our kids and families. Both are important. Every minute we pull disciples out of the community onto the church campus, we pull them off the mission field. At the same time, every minute disciples are on the church campus should strengthen them and motivate them to live faithfully in the community.

This all means that we might need to seek a better balance for our families and encourage them to do many of the things we tend to discourage. It might even mean we need to do less on campus to give our church—our families—the room to do more. We don't have to see public schools, extracurricular sports (even travel ball), family vacations, band camps, and so many other activities as "secular" distractions standing in opposition to the "sacred." Instead, we can see these as good gifts that God intended our families to enjoy and as potential evangelism launching mission activities. If we are doing our job as disciple-making disciples, then we can jettison the fears of our families abandoning the church. We don't abandon that which we love and cherish. Remember, love always prompts behavior.

Different discipleship methods and programs have come and gone. Some were great; others were fads. Some helped advance Christ's kingdom; others may have had minimal effect. New methods and programs will come and go. But the one thing that must always stay the same is why we are discipling—to help kids (1) know Jesus, (2) love Jesus, and (3) live like Jesus. Nothing else is more important.

So, what's the one thing you need most to disciple your kids today? That's easy. Jesus. [period]

[LIVING IT OUT]

- *What new or ongoing challenges to discipling kids do you believe are most dangerous today?*

- *Which aspect of the discipleship triad of knowing, loving, or living is your ministry best at? Which could be better?*

- *How do you view your kids' and families' participation in your community: as a threat or an opportunity? Why?*

JESUS FOR TODAY
APOLOGETICS AND WORLDVIEW

Valerie Bell

[
But in your hearts revere Christ as Lord. Always be
prepared to give an answer to everyone who asks you to
give the reason for the hope that you have.
But do this with gentleness and respect.
-1 Peter 3:15
]

It's a strange memory, I admit. Maybe that's why it has stuck with me all these years. I am three years old, and I am with my aunt—my beautiful, bleached blonde, bejeweled, Hollywood-glamorous, childless aunt. She is my mother's younger sister. She has dressed me up in a white rabbit fur coat and curled my towhead hair like Shirley Temple. All this makes me look like my aunt's "mini me," which, through the years, I have come to understand was the whole point!

Strangely, I am standing on a bar counter, looking out over a restaurant of smiling adult faces turned my way.

97

On top of that, I am singing.

Beyond strange…the lyrics of the song are a child's questions to her mother about what her future will be like when she grows up.

In the song, the mother answers her child's questions: "Who knows about the future? It will be what it will be."

Someone has described this very popular 50's song "as a heaping dose of cheerful fatalism." Cheerful fatalism! What a blend of adjective and noun. I can promise you that my three-year-old self didn't have a clue what I was singing about.

When I finish, the restaurant applauds. Then, the strangest thing of all happens… my aunt starts talking from the bar counter to the whole restaurant.

"Thank you! Thank you! Yes, my daughter, Valerie, is just three years old. Can you believe it?"

"Oh yes! Music runs in our family. My daughter got it from my father. She has perfect pitch!"

Well, well, well…I knew I didn't have perfect pitch and I especially knew I wasn't **her daughter**! What was going on here?

But despite the lies, I am feeling very loved and wanted… and certain I had better not report all of this to my parents!

My parents—my dad was a voice professor and Chairman of the Music Department at Moody Bible Institute, and my mom was a Christian author. Had they known about this, they would not have approved. That's because my aunt and my parents didn't see life in the same way. Their philosophies of life, and their views of God all evolved from different perceptions—or totally different worldviews.

My aunt was attractively secular. She embraced life. She loved people, including me. She was artistic—her home often won community contests for best-decorated house for the holidays. She took me to movies—like "50 Leagues Under the Sea"—which was unthinkable in my parents' home. When I stayed with my aunt over the weekends, we went to horse races and county fairs, kiddylands and swimming pools. We wore matching perfume and nail polish. Everywhere we went, I was her pretend, but beloved "daughter."

But though my parents shared some of my aunt's love of life, my aunt's worldview held to a very different perspective of God than that of my parents. To my aunt, He was distant and very undefined. She wasn't an atheist, but God only received a nod of her head. Without realizing it, her life was built around what amounted to a lie—that God was rarely involved in human life. My aunt's worldview included the belief that good people went to heaven, so we should all try to be good then. Her beliefs were basically her own construct.

It will be what it will be. Cheerful fatalism. That could have been her life theme song. It described her worldview.

In his book, *The Problem of Pain*, C.S. Lewis describes why people sometimes choose to view God as distant.

> We want not so much a Father, but a grandfather in heaven, a God who said of anything we happened to like doing, "What does it matter so long as they are contented?"

My parents held to a very different worldview than Lewis described above. Their young lives had been scarred by parental alcoholism, abandonment, and death. Fortunately, they had been radically saved as young adults and, for the first time, they had found security and stability. My mother's Bible was worn and underlined. We prayed together. We attended First Baptist Church at least three times a week where my father was the Minister of Music and my mother organized

Vacation Bible Schools and backyard Bible Clubs. On Sunday nights, I went to bed lullabied from the music in our living room where the "church aunts and uncles" gathered to sing together while my dad accompanied them on the piano.

> Amazing grace! How sweet the sound
> That saved a wretch like me!
> I once was lost, but now am found;
> Was blind, but now I see.

My parents' worldview was biblical—Christ-centered, missional, and devoted to the church and the truth of Scripture. God was near us and for us. We sensed it.

But my beloved aunt? My beautiful, loving aunt? I'm pretty sure she never embraced Jesus like my parents had.

Truthfully, it may have been hard for her to see Jesus. Why? Without intending to, I'm afraid we hid Him behind a certain kind of "spiritual scaffolding" built around us that supported what we understood to be the truth of Scripture. These "extras" were there to help Christians like us live discipled lives in a secular world.

But the very "scaffolding" meant to strengthen us, most likely got in the way, built a barrier and hid Jesus. We were the no-dancing, no-drinking, no-card-playing, no-theatre, no-movies, no-bowling alley-or-poolhall, no-makeup, no-rock-music evangelicals. That was LOUD and CLEAR! Jesus, sadly, was hidden behind what was more apparent… our form of legalistic religion embraced by our church culture during my growing up years.

I'm convinced that's what my aunt saw and why she worked so hard to "convert" me to her worldview. She must have thought that everything she loved would have to be stripped away for her to become a Christ-follower. I believe the "scaffolding" was too hard a pill for her to swallow and why I don't believe she ever found Jesus as her personal Savior.

Scaffolding isn't all wrong, but we need to recognize that it can promote religion more than it promotes faith. Scaffolding has "in-the-club" rules. Scaffolding complicates the understanding of the gospel. Legalistic scaffolding practices may sometimes even substitute for actual faith.

But most tragically, scaffolding hides Jesus, as if Jesus is not enough.

In his recent book, *Not in It to Win It*, Andy Stanley expresses the wonder of the power of Jesus. Speaking of Christianity's roots:

> Against all odds, a cult dedicated to a crucified teacher with no territory, military, or recognized authority survived, multiplied, and eventually replaced the prevailing...not religion. Christianity replaced the prevailing worldview.
>
> Think of it: Jesus didn't only change the lives of believers for the better, (though he certainly did that) but he impacted how the entire world looked at life—he changed the global worldview. Even the secular world was deeply shaped by Christianity. Jesus changed how the world lived.

Because of Jesus...

Children were thought of differently. Through Christians rescuing little babies from death by exposure, the world evolved to understand the horror and abuse of allowing a baby's death by weather and nature. The value of children was raised all over the world—in European homes, in Asian homes, African and American homes... homes everywhere. Children around the world would have safer lives because of Jesus' love...whether they knew Him or not.

The list goes on.

Because of Jesus…

Practices like human sacrifice would come to be thought of as too vile a supposed remedy even for pagans and their blood-thirsty pagan gods. Jesus would become the "ultimate sacrifice" eliminating the price of satisfying God with human blood. What a deliverance that gospel message brought to the world!

Because of Jesus…

Women were thought of more highly and were recognized as having equal inherent value. *"The origins of this principle… lay not in the French Revolution, nor in the Declaration of Independence, nor in the Enlightenment, but in the Bible… In Rome men did not hesitate to use slaves and prostitutes to relieve themselves of their sexual needs. The idea that every woman had the right to choose what happened to her body was laughable."*[1]

Jesus' respect for women raised them to be more than sexual objects.

Because of Jesus…

Learning was more appreciated and highly reverenced. Jesus, himself, was a highly effective teacher. Scripture says, *"…people were hanging on every word he spoke..."* (Luke 19:48 MSG)

Because of Jesus…

Humility, charity, love for others… the myriad of Christian virtues became admired and emulated.

---

1   *Jesus Changed Everything for Women* The Gospel Coalition March 22, 2021 Rebecca McLaughlin

In John Ortberg's book *Who is This Man,* John quotes Yale historian Jaroslav Pelikan's observation about Jesus' place in history:

> Regardless of what you may personally think about him, Jesus of Nazareth has been the dominant figure in the history of Western Culture for almost 20 centuries.

Impressive. Although Jesus' influence is often taken for granted or ignored today, it cannot be denied.

But that's history, someone may be thinking. What about today's secular worldview? Does Jesus have much to say to today's world? And what is the secular perspective that today's Christians must address?

A revealing 2005 study by sociologist Christian Smith examined the beliefs of teenagers from a variety of backgrounds. In most cases, teenagers adhered to a "mushy" pseudo religion he called Moralistic Therapeutic Deism or MTD.

MTD has five tenets:

- A God exists who created and orders the world and watches over human life on earth.
- God wants people to be good, nice, and fair to each other as taught in the Bible and most of the religions of the world.
- The central goal in life is to be happy and to feel good about yourself.
- God does not need to be involved in one's life except when needed to resolve a problem.
- Good people go to heaven when they die.

Does this sound familiar? It does to me. I hear the echo of my aunt's worldview in those five points. The future "will be what it will be" so try to do good and be happy. Being happy is the main thing, after all. This belief system definitely reflects a human preference for a "...*grandfather God who thinks, 'What does it matter, so long as they are contented?'*"

Cheerful fatalism.

Additionally, these five widely believed MTD tenets follow no religious philosophy, historic wisdom, or proven practice. It is wholly self-constructed. It contains some seeds of truth but amounts to misinformation and all this misinformation is actually lies.

Today's secular worldview is designed to make us feel good about ourselves.

- Believe in yourself.
- You be you!
- Live your truth.
- Follow your heart.
- My body, my choice.
- Good vibe tribe.
- You are enough.

Tim Keller describes such a worldview and resulting lifestyle as "unchecked expressive individualism."

Unchecked expressive individualism also means that no one is seen as a "sinner" anymore and therefore the concept of salvation or redemption is irrelevant.

And Jesus? He is perceived as a historical figure no longer needed. Everyone is good enough without a Savior. Any sense of spiritual need is dampened, and Jesus is no longer seen as the Messiah, the Son of the living God. **Today's worldview is that humans need acceptance, not repentance. That's what love looks like now.**

Today's seemingly empathetic message to "sinners" is You be You.

When I think of the prevalent worldview today, I think the humble hope in the words of John Newton's hymn, Amazing Grace, may be particularly needed for today:

> I once was lost, but now am found.
> Was blind but now I see.

Why does today's secular worldview so strongly lean towards empathy? It is well-intended cheerful fatalism. Hope for change is gone, so acceptance must be offered. In fact, acceptance and empathy are often demanded in our world today.

But empathy, in fact, may be the cruelest approach of all when change is actually possible and desperately needed. The Bible makes it clear that God is intimately involved in our lives. Page after page tells the stories of centuries of redeemed lives. The Bible speaks to our deep need for hope for better, stronger, and resilient lives - for eternal lives. We can be confident that our heavenly Father is miraculously involved with us.

How sad to leave people with a sinful cancer rotting within because we are fatalistic about their hope for change.

How sad to ignore an addict chained to his or her compulsive needs forever because we don't have the spiritual fortitude to walk him or her through deliverance.

How sad to never know the forgiving love of God, the understanding compassion of Jesus, or the guidance of the Holy Spirit. To grieve without hope. To never experience mystery, or spiritual community, or the presence of God is a life of diminished existence. Such lives are lived in the most severe poverty and deprivation.

Think of it… our hearts should be broken for anyone living without an intimate relationship with Jesus.

What a loss to never have stood shoulder to shoulder with other believers while singing your testament to the wonder of God's work in your lives.

You've been here. The tears have flowed! Your soul has risen to express this truth with others:

> Amazing grace! How sweet the sound
> That saved a wretch like me!
> I once was lost, but now am found;
> Was blind, but now I see.

I heard a "sermon" in a most unlikely place recently. It made tears of gratitude run down my cheeks. I was on my way to visit my son in Pasadena, California and decided to Uber from LAX airport to his home to save him some hassle and some time. But I had second thoughts about my decision when, after collecting my luggage, I realized it wasn't as simple as using my Uber app - walking out to the curb and grabbing my ride. No, I needed to walk a long way dragging my luggage behind me to the shuttle pick-up location, where I would wait 15 minutes for the shuttle. I would then load my luggage with a crowd competing for luggage space and get dropped off at a station to line up behind scores of others needing rides with taxi and Ubers.

By the time my ride pulled up, I was second-guessing my decision. It didn't comfort me when his car turned out to be a beat-up old Toyota, but I reassured myself that his driver rating was high. But, I admit, I was intrepid.

Because of COVID, all the windows of my driver's car were open. He wore a mask. His accent was foreign.

"Where are you from?" I asked, trying to make small talk.

"I'm from Eritrea."

He was surprised, delighted actually, that I had heard of that small country that is a neighbor to Ethiopia.

I told him I worked for a Christian ministry to children that was active in 132 countries of the world.

That did it! He was thrilled I was a believer. He called me "sister" as he shared his life story.

Christians are persecuted in Eritrea. Christians are murdered in Eritrea. Sixteen years ago, after the murder of his Christian business partner by the government of Eritrea; my driver had to flee for his life from his homeland. He left with nothing. No passport. No money. Then shortly after he fled, his daughter and her boyfriend were imprisoned for praying together in her home—an illegal act. She has spent most of her child-bearing years behind bars—13 years! Recently she was released and will soon be married to her also recently released boyfriend. My driver will probably never see them again in this lifetime. His Uber driving helps support them.

He could have been broken, bitter or disappointed with God. But no! His story was told punctuated by his faith. "God can do anything! All we must do is have faith!" "God can move mountains. Do you believe that sister?"

I am so lifted by his faith, that a thought crosses my mind, *perhaps he is a plant from God, an angelic visitor, someone sent my way to challenge my sagging faith.*

Soon I can't hold back. I am now joining in his faith celebration. I say, "Amen!" smiling at him and "Preach it brother!" and "Praise God!"

Pretty good for a Baptist, don't you think?

With our windows wide open in L.A. rush hour traffic, we are listening to the local Christian radio station, K-Love, and singing our hearts out together with the music.

People are staring at us. It's alright. I'm used to singing in strange places, being stared at while someone's calling me their daughter or sister. It all works for me!

And what really works for me is believing that Jesus' life still rocks our world. And this is why:

> *For God so loved the world that He gave his only Son...*
> *-John 3:16*

> *I give you a new commandment: love one another.*
> *-John 13:34*

Considering all of this, what should we do? What can we do?

Let me suggest some specific next steps.

We must begin by examining the scaffolding that is obscuring Jesus in our time and then bravely begin to dismantle it. Jesus would be more obvious in our world if He was incarnate in those who are his followers.

What if we were so faith-filled that, for the sake of a lost world, we would:

- Tame our righteous anger when lost people behave like they're lost. Consider that the scaffolding that declares war on our culture hides Jesus. I'm convinced we should declare love instead.

- Remove the yard signs, the bumper stickers, and the tee-shirts that demonstrate a competing loyalty to Jesus. Be politically active, speak up—go Republican or Democratic—fine...but don't hide Jesus! Is He our primary allegiance? Do our neighbors know that?
- Stop our attacks, our name-calling, and disrespect for those who disagree with us on social media and in other public arenas. Instead, we should focus our passion and energies on understanding and loving like Jesus.
- Make sure our children and grandchildren have a front-row seat to what faith actually looks like. Has our "talk" been focused on politics, economies, echoes of our preferred news channels, and stock market losses? What if our faith held strong regardless of our circumstances? What if "faith talk" was primary these days? Do our families know our God stories and how God has moved mountains in our lives? What if we dared to believe God can still move the new mountains we face and that **He is** *for* **us**. What if our families saw that kind of faith in us?

Then we would be beautiful.

We would be humble.

We would love like Jesus.

We would roll our car windows down and sing out our faith to the world at the top of our lungs. Well...maybe something similar anyway.

Oh that we would dare to believe that Jesus could still rock our world and change today's worldview for the better! Jesus is the world changer. Do we still believe it?

In the Sermon on the Mount, Jesus gave a blueprint for Christ-followers to practice.

THE SERMON ON THE MOUNT—
THE BEATITUDES

Now when Jesus saw the crowds, He went up on the mountain; and after He sat down, His disciples came to Him. And He opened His mouth and began to teach them, saying,

"Blessed are the poor in spirit, for theirs is the kingdom of heaven.

Blessed are those who mourn, for they will be comforted.

Blessed are the gentle, for they will inherit the earth.

Blessed are those who hunger and thirst for righteousness, for they will be satisfied.

Blessed are the merciful, for they will receive mercy.

Blessed are the pure in heart, for they will see God.

Blessed are the peacemakers, for they will be called sons of God.

Blessed are those who have been persecuted for the sake of righteousness, for theirs is the kingdom of heaven.

Blessed are you when people insult you and persecute you, and falsely say all kinds of evil against you because of Me. Rejoice and be glad, for your reward in heaven is great; for in this same way they persecuted the prophets who were before you.

You are the salt of the earth; but if the salt has become tasteless, how can it be made salty again? It is no longer good for anything, except to be thrown out and trampled underfoot by people.

You are the light of the world. A city set on a hill cannot be hidden; nor do people light a lamp and put it under a basket, but on the lampstand, and it gives light to all who are in the house. Your light must shine before people in such a way that they may see your good works and glorify your Father who is in heaven."- Matthew 5:3-16 (NASB)

Jesus is all. He is more than enough. He is still the world-changer.

He is the image of the invisible God, the firstborn of all creation:

for by Him all things were created, both in the heavens and on earth, visible and invisible, whether thrones, or dominions, or rulers, or authorities—all things have been created through Him and for Him.

He is before all things, and in Him all things hold together. He is also the head of the body, the church; and He is the beginning, the firstborn from the dead, so that He Himself will come to have first place in everything.

For it was the Father's good pleasure for all the fullness to dwell in Him, and through Him to reconcile all things to Himself, whether things on earth or things in [heaven, having made peace through the blood of His cross. -Colossians 1:15-20 (NASB)

It is so much more than a promise to be fulfilled in the future. It should be at the core of our DNA for those who walk with Jesus and know Him personally. It is far from a power-based, argumentative, raised-fist worldview. They are Jesus' expectations for us, to be like him. Jesus. [period]

LIVING IT OUT

- *What scaffolding have you experienced in your Christian walk?*

- *What does Jesus have to say to the world today?*

- *What is the lie this worldview embraces?*

JESUS IS THE ANSWER

HANDLING DIFFICULT TOPICS: JESUS, JUSTICE, AND INJUSTICE

Guylando and Esther Moreno

On one occasion an expert in the law stood up to test Jesus. "Teacher," he asked, "what must I do to inherit eternal life?" "What is written in the Law?" he replied. "How do you read it?"

He answered, "'Love the Lord your God with all your heart and with all your soul and with all your strength and with all your mind'[a]; and, 'Love your neighbor as yourself.'"

"You have answered correctly," Jesus replied. "Do this and you will live."

But he wanted to justify himself, so he asked Jesus, "And who is my neighbor?"

In reply Jesus said: "A man was going down from Jerusalem

to Jericho, when he was attacked by robbers. They stripped him of his clothes, beat him and went away, leaving him half dead. A priest happened to be going down the same road, and when he saw the man, he passed by on the other side. So too, a Levite, when he came to the place and saw him, passed by on the other side. But a Samaritan, as he traveled, came where the man was; and when he saw him, he took pity on him. He went to him and bandaged his wounds, pouring on oil and wine. Then he put the man on his own donkey, brought him to an inn and took care of him. The next day he took out two denarii and gave them to the innkeeper. 'Look after him,' he said, 'and when I return, I will reimburse you for any extra expense you may have.'

"Which of these three do you think was a neighbor to the man who fell into the hands of robbers?"

The expert in the law replied, "The one who had mercy on him."

Jesus told him, "Go and do likewise."
-Luke 10:25-37

In a world where there are so many counterfeit claims for justice, how can you be certain that your life and ministry reflect the Biblical definition of justice?

In our increasingly politically polarized world, cries for "justice" have become all too common. In every major city, there are protests, marches, and demonstrations where people's claims for justice cover all manner of social angst. From gun rights to abortion rights, we often find ourselves and our ministries at the epicenter of cultural debates – all purporting to seek justice for some type of aggrieved offense. But who's definition of justice should prevail? Complicating matters further, not only are we called to elevate God's definition of justice, but must do so in such a way that children can understand. Given all of the counterfeit claims for justice, it is imperative that the next generation be able to distinguish between the world and the Word's definition of justice.

Thankfully, Jesus, the Author and Finisher of our faith has provided his timeless truth to equip both leaders and children to discern justice from injustice. In the parable of the good Samaritan, Jesus illustrates the Biblical definition of justice. A justice that is rooted in the twin aims of: (1) loving the *"Lord your God with all your heart, with all your soul, with all your strength, and with all your mind,"* and (2) loving *"your neighbor as yourself"* (Luke 10:27 NIV). A justice that is selfless, sacrificial, and extends beyond cultural boundaries to care for the weak, marginalized, and oppressed. A justice so motivated by love and compassion that it shames the religious elite, but brings glory to God through good works. A justice that is not blinded by self-serving definitions of what is right in one's own eyes, but is grounded in God's standard of righteousness. Apart from these scriptural guideposts, our children could easily succumb to prevailing cultural norms instead of timeless Biblical truth.

Today's children's ministry leader must not shy away from the injustices that permeate our culture, but must lean into them with the truth and grace of the Gospel. If we ignore these issues, then we are no better than the priest and Levite who passed by the man who was stripped and beaten by robbers. Rather, we must teach our children to *"act justly and to love mercy and to walk humbly with [their] God."* Albeit daunting, we must explain justice and injustice in age-appropriate ways so that children will recognize and act accordingly when they are older. Believe it or not, children are often highly sensitive to concepts of fairness and equality. While these larger questions of injustice may challenge their young minds, more common examples are a lot more accessible to them. Cheating on a math test, sharing of snacks, or how you treat someone who is different are all vehicles to introduce these concepts in ways that children can more easily digest. Drawing on your children's own feelings of hurt, rejection, or unjust treatment are steppingstones to Jesus' treatment for caring for the least of these. An everyday fight over a favorite toy can quickly become a masterclass on the golden rule of treating others the way we want to be treated. We must never neglect the power of practical application because these lessons will serve as seeds of truth that will, in due season, blossom into trees of righteousness in their little hearts and minds.

Yet one of our most powerful tools is to serve as living examples by modeling justice in our own lives. How do you treat the poor, marginalized, and oppressed? How does your faith motivate you toward compassion? In what ways have you been a good Samaritan this week? In so doing, you will serve as a modern-day, living example of God's righteous standard at work in a world that has lost its way. God's justice will always align with God's Word. God's justice always bends toward righteous living. God's justice models Christ's heart for the outcast, widow, and orphan. God's justice loves a neighbor just as much as it loves itself. If we are to be effective at transmitting this truth to the next generation, then there is no better way than to embody it ourselves.

When confronted with claims of injustice, our only recourse is to measure them against Biblical truth. Only then will we – and the children we are called to serve – know when it is time to engage in ways that reflect God and his sacrificial love. Our faith is not one that recoils or turns a blind eye to injustice. Yet it is one that seeks to restore justice by modeling it before a generation of children poised to do the same.

So how can you be certain that your life and ministry reflect the Biblical definition of justice? Jesus. [period]

[LIVING IT OUT]

- *Why is it important to distinguish the world's definition of justice from God's definition?*

- *In what ways can you illustrate God's heart for justice in your Children's Ministry?*

- *How does your personal life reflect God's heart for justice?*

JESUS IS THE ANSWER

HANDLING DIFFICULT TOPICS: TECH, DIGITAL MEDIA, AND FORMATION

Team RaiseUpFaith

[
Set your minds on things above, not on earthly things.
-Colossians 3:2
]

Think back to when you were a child, to your time at school or Sunday School. What was it like? Perhaps you remember gathering around your teacher as he or she read stories from a big book and passed around the pictures. Maybe you had something more technologically advanced – an enormous TV that was wheeled into the classroom to show Bible cartoons on video tapes.

Even only a couple of decades ago, life and learning looked very different to how it does now. Twenty-first century kids have been born into a fully-fledged, hi-tech, digital world – a world of internet and personal handheld digital devices. And it's one they engage with from an early age. A 2018 Ofcom report found that 36% of 3-4-year-olds in the UK play games online for around 6 hours a week. 45% watch YouTube – 8 in 10 use it to watch cartoons, and 4 in 10 to watch funny videos. Over half of pre-schoolers (52%) go online for around 9 hours a week. A recent report from Common Sense Media found that in 2021, screen time for the average US tween was around five and one-half hours a day. For US teenagers, that increased to eight and one-half.[1]

Some two thousand years or so ago, Paul encouraged the Christians in Colossae to "set [their] mind on the things that are above, not on the things that are on earth" (Colossians 3:2). As kidmin leaders, we're following in this great and wonderful tradition of helping our children to see Jesus, so that they may love him and respond to his invitation to follow him. Over two millennia, the mission and the message remain the same; but the method and the media – how we do it and the resources we use – need to be relevant to our time.

As kidmin leaders, we need to keep in mind the reality of today's hi-tech, digital world as we disciple our children. It's not just that our ministry is enhanced by using digital media...it's vital. After all, this is the language our children speak. They're used to learning through audio-visual media, and discovering through digital devices. It makes sense for us to help children engage with Scripture and learn about Jesus in ways that make sense to them. It's important that we engage with digital media well as we teach our kids. But we also need to help our kids engage with it well beyond the classroom. Research in the UK found that by the time the average young person is 18, he or she will have spent 35,000 hours on media. That compares to 9,000 hours in school, 2,500 hours engaging with their parents, and 900 hours in

---

1   Children and Parents: Media Use and Attitudes Report 2018 – Ofcom

church. In other words, that's just under 4 years on media 24 hours a day, 7 days a week, compared to just over 1 month in church. There's an ever-growing world online that our kids are exploring on a daily, even hourly, basis.[2]

It's striking what a noisy place the internet is. And, it's almost impossible to visit that space for any length of time and not be impacted by what you hear and what you see. We must learn to discern what's good, and true, and life-giving from what isn't - the things from "above" versus the things "on earth". It's useful to ask, how do some of these online places make us feel about ourselves? About our neighbor? If they end up making us feel less loved and less loving, then they're not helping us set our minds on "the things that are above" because, as Jesus said, the highest priority is love - for our Heavenly Father and for others (Matthew 22:37-40).

We need to ask these questions of ourselves, first of all. If we want Jesus to be the center of our ministry, then he needs to be the center of our lives – including our digital habits. If we want a healthy ministry, then we need to be feeding our mind and soul with stuff which is good for us and for our relationship with Jesus. Then we can help our kids do the same. Practically speaking, this looks like firstly auditing our own habits, keeping track of what we are engaging in, and being mindful of how it affects our thought lives. It's from this position that we can have the authority to learn about what our kids are watching and playing online, and who they're following; and to offer Jesus-centered insights into what they're experiencing, and inevitably learning, beyond the walls of the church classroom.

Let's harness the potential, too. Today's digital technology provides awesome opportunities for nurturing our children's everyday relationship with Jesus. It's never been easier to share and connect – and very often, it doesn't cost a thing! So, let's look out for digital ministry

---

2 The Common Sense Census: Media Use by Tweens and Teens (2021) - Common Sense Media

content providers, as well as those great devotional apps created for our kids' age and stage. We must take the lead in introducing them to online content that will encourage, excite, and inspire them in their walk with Jesus.

In the twenty-first century, there are more questions than ever. Thanks to our online culture, there are more answers, too. However, in today's hi-tech, digital world, the eternal truth remains the same.

It's our job as kidmin leaders, in the media saturated world that our kids live in, to show them the source of truth, to teach them not only how to spot truth (filtering out the noise and garbage) but how to stand on the truth. Now more than ever, the world is fighting for our kids - Satan is fighting for their attention and for their eternity. We need to show them truth.

The answer is Jesus. [period]

[LIVING IT OUT]

- *How do you/could you use digital content in your ministry – in the classroom and beyond – to help children on their journey with Jesus?*

- *Think about your own 'digital diet.' Does it nourish you and bring you closer to Jesus? Is there anything you might need to cut down on?*

- *How well do you understand the digital culture your children and young people experience?*

JESUS IS THE ANSWER

HANDLING DIFFICULT TOPICS: ANXIETY

Abby Koontz

[
Having cast all your anxiety on Him,
because He cares about you.
-1 Peter 5:7
]

Billy Graham has said "Historians will probably call our era 'the age of anxiety.' Anxiety is the natural result when our hopes are centered in anything short of God and His will for us." Anxiety in children (and adults for that matter) has been on the rise since the 1950's. There are several factors creating this trend including lack of security coinciding with the breakdown of the family unit and now supercharged by social media. It can seem like an overwhelming burden for us to shoulder, let alone our children. And yet, the Bible calls us to be anxious about nothing (Philippians 4:6). Surely this is not possible? Surely, in writing to the Philippians, Paul was just unaware of the "age of anxiety" Billy Graham notes we are now living in! And still we know those He has called He has equipped. Hebrews 13:20-21 says, *"Now may the God of peace, who brought up from the dead the great Shepherd of the sheep through the blood of the eternal covenant, that is, Jesus our Lord, equip you in every good thing to do His will, working in us that which is pleasing in His sight, through Jesus Christ, to whom be the glory forever and ever. Amen."* What a beautiful and powerful benediction. Death and the power of death has been defeated and we can have the peace of God because of the sacrifice of Jesus. This verse is such a precious reminder that our answer to this seemingly ludicrous goal of being anxious for nothing is… Jesus. Jesus is, in fact, both the example, and also, the means by which we can achieve freedom from anxiety.

I encourage you to meditate on one antidote for anxiety…. Trust. Please understand, I do not wish to minimize the experience of anxiety by simply stating "trust more", but we do know the One who is all together trustworthy, and He desires what is best for us. His yoke is light. We can encourage our own hearts and the hearts of the children we serve with this truth. Let's look closer at Jesus' sacrifice which brings us freedom and at a specific time during that sacrifice where He displays great trust in an excruciating experience.

Some of us were taught or have taught our children the prayer "Now I lay me down to sleep. I pray the Lord my soul to keep". Well, in Jesus' day children were taught a bedtime prayer as well. Psalm 31:5 says in part, *"Into your hand I commit my spirit."* This is a night-time prayer used in Jewish tradition. It is likely Jesus was also taught this prayer. And we never want to read too much into the text, but it is possible that he also had the preceding portion of the Psalm on his mind as he uttered his last words on the cross. Psalm 31:1-5 says *"In You, O LORD, I have taken refuge; Let me never be ashamed; In Your righteousness deliver me. Incline Your ear to me, rescue me quickly; Be to me a rock of strength, A stronghold to save me. For You are my rock and my fortress; For Your name's sake You will lead me and guide me. You will pull me out of the net which they have secretly laid for me, For You are my strength. Into Your hand I commit my spirit; You have ransomed me, O LORD, God of truth.*" Christ's statement on the cross is really an echo of Psalm 31:5 and can be understood in a similar sense, as an expression of trust in God in even extreme circumstances. Jesus shows us how to utilize trust to navigate even the most colossal anxiety producing circumstances. We can certainly apply the same trust in the Father and His character, strength, omniscience, and love for us to combat our day-to-day struggles with anxiety.

There is an old sermon illustration, at least as old as the mid 1800's, about a botanist in the highlands of Scotland who spotted a rare and highly prized plant far below the cliff where he stood on a little embankment jutting out from the sheer cliff face. As he stood there contemplating how he could get down to the embankment to retrieve the plant, a little Scottish boy came walking along. The botanist stopped the boy, pointed to the plant far below, and explained the situation. "I wonder," he asked the boy, "if you will allow me to tie my rope around your waste and lower you down to the plant? I promise I will not let you go." The boy heard the proposal, paused, looked back over the edge of the cliff, and said, "No." As he turned to go, the now frantic botanist called for the boy to stop, produced his wallet, and offered the boy an impressive sum of money. "I will pay you," he said, "if you will let me lower you down." The boy paused again. He looked at the money, looked back over the cliff edge at the plant far below, looked back at the man, thought for a bit, and then said, "I'll tell you what, mister. I don't want your money. And I'm not going to let you lower me down there. But I will do it for free if you meet one demand." "Anything," the botanist said. "I will do it," replied the boy, "if my father can hold the rope."

Trust. Jesus was exemplifying trust in His Father in the most agonizing of moments. Take a minute and think about who you trust, who you really trust? There is probably one common theme in those each of us trust. We know that individual; we have spent time with that individual; we have learned to trust that individual based on their characteristics, their reliability, and their care for us. We must teach the children we serve to know who God is and experience Him and in so doing trust Him and His heart for them because as I Peter 5:7 says, We *"can cast all our anxiety on Him because He cares for us."*

We can trust the Father who loves us when it comes to death, and we can also trust Him with all our struggles and challenges in life because as the Psalm states He is our rock and our fortress. Thank God there is a refuge from the storms of life and from the terrors of death. The refuge is in the Father's hand. It is our faith that we are in the Father's hand. That is truly a refuge. Jesus exemplifies this trust for us and also provides the power to live and breathe in that trust. How can we possibly have freedom from the crushing weight of anxiety? Jesus. [period]

[LIVING IT OUT]

- *What anxieties do you need to lay at the feet of the Father?*

- *In your ministry, how can you teach children how to be free from the weight of anxiety?*

- *What steps will you take to lead children into a place of trust with with Father?*

JESUS IS THE ANSWER
HANDLING DIFFICULT TOPICS: IDENTITY

Cindy Bultema: GEMS Girls' Clubs

[
See how great a love the Father has given us,
that we would be called children of God; and in fact we are
-1 John 3:1a
]

You are a ministry leader. It's what you do, and it matters.

As a ministry leader, you may know what it is to have ministry permeate your calendar, consume your thoughts, and drive your ambitions to the point that your ministry shifts from what you do to who you are. Ministry can become your identity, the way you introduce yourself, and the name tag you wear: "Hello, My Name is Children's Ministry Leader."

Though you are a hero of faith, if your identity is centered on anything outside of Jesus—even children's ministry—you have an identity crisis. I know this thanks to my friend Jen.

Within an hour of Jen sitting at my kitchen table, I had filled her with two cups of coffee and an earful of lies.

"I'm a disaster; I'm fat, I'm disappointing everyone, I'm..."

That's when Jen placed her coffee mug on the table with a thunk, leaned in, and asked, "Cindy, who said that to you?"

Her question stopped me mid-sentence.

Compelled by love, she pressed for an answer, "Really, Cindy, who said that to you?"

My thoughts rolled back through two decades, countless voices, and one high school bathroom stall.

Scrawled on the chipped bathroom wall of the girls' restroom were six words.

"Cindy is a fat red cow."

Those words pierced when I was fifteen, and unfortunately, were still adhered to me like a sticky name tag. "Hello, my name is Cindy. I'm a fat red cow."

Now much had changed since that dreadful high school day. The restroom had new paint; I had new friends like Jen; and most importantly, I had surrendered my life to Jesus. I was now a Jesus-loving girl on mission, telling anyone who will listen how He set me free. All that was old was made new! He gave me a new identity and new names.

Yet, here I was stuck in old muck. The lies hadn't lost their stick!

I wonder if you can relate? Have you surrendered your life, but not your labels? Maybe you're wearing name tags that read, "Hello, My Name Is…Not Enough, Rejected, Inadequate, or Unloved?" Or maybe you're wearing ministry name tags tied to your position, your successes or failures, or the number of children or volunteers in your ministry?

If that's your story, here's my question. "Friend, who said that to you?"

Who told you that you're not good enough, rejected, inadequate, or maybe even unloved? Who told you that your worth is based on the opinions of others, the size of your budget, or the number of heads counted each Sunday?

It wasn't Jesus! The voice of Jesus is love, and His words are always Truth.

Jesus not only receives us, but He also frees us. He sets us free from lies, labels, and name tags that may wound, but were never meant to stick.

He teaches us in His Word how to live "set free". Ephesians 4:22-24 says to rid yourselves of the old self… and to put on the new self, which *in the likeness* of God has been created in righteousness and holiness of the truth.

Here's the thing. Lies don't fall off; they are taken off. We must choose to peel them off one by one with His Truth.

The Truth is that Jesus has named you from "A" to "Z." You are "A"—Accepted. Your worth does not come from parental accolades or ministry accomplishments. You "B"—Belong. You belong to God and you matter to your ministry team. "C"—Chosen. God picked you and gifted you. You are the leader He can use to make an eternal difference in the lives of this generation! "D"—Delivered. He delivered you from old patterns, lies, and habits and made you new! To "Z"—Zealous for God. He is why you are so passionate that this generation knows Jesus!

After Jen's question, I got back to the basics, A-B-C style. And of all the Truth-filled names He's given me, I have this one on repeat: "L"— *Loved. Loved. Period.* Yes, I add a period to loved. I am loved, no matter what! No matter how I feel, or how many kids showed up on Sunday morning, if I'm making my quarterly goals, or what anyone scrawls on the bathroom stall. I am Loved. Period.

Friend, so are you. When old name tags start to stick to your new life, remember that you always have a choice to where you bend your ear. And Jesus says you are seen, known, and so very LOVED. [Period]

Your identity can hold you back:

- I'm terrible at communicating with adults.
- I don't have enough money, time, or resources.
- I'm disappointing everyone.

Or your identity can be Jesus-centered and Truth-filled:

- I am qualified (Colossians 1:12).
- I am enough and I have enough (2 Peter 1:3).
- I am LOVED (1 John 3:1).

What you choose will change everything for you and for your kids.

As you choose to believe who God says you are, it will filter into how you teach and how you lead. You are leading wonderfully made, children of God. They are loved by the Father. They are accepted. They belong. They are chosen. When you begin to shift your thinking, your whole mindset changes. Those voices speaking lies will get more and more quiet.

That unruly child that has trouble listening, she is an image bearer of God. The parent that causes problems and questions everything you do, he is a child of God.

Put off the lies and put on the truth God declares, for the kids and parents in your ministry, your volunteers, and especially yourself.

Friend, as you plan, prepare, and pour into kids and your ministry team; declare your Truth-filled identity. Remind your soul: I am a Child of God, Seen, Known, Enough, and so Loved. What you do matters, but it does not define you. Your Truth-filled identity is in Jesus. [period]

LIVING IT OUT

- *When introducing yourself, how do you finish this sentence, "Hello, I am _____." Does your answer reflect your Truth-filled identity in Christ?*

- *What child needs you to ask, "Who said that to you?" Then choose a way to share this today: "You are Loved. Period."*

- *Listen to the voices speaking to you. If it's a lie, ask God to help you "put it off." (And if it's too sticky, phone a prayer friend.) "Put on" Truth by declaring you are Loved. Period.*

JESUS IN THE CLASSROOM
BRINGING THE BIBLE TO LIFE

Courtney Weaver

> For the word of God is alive and active. Sharper than any double-edged sword, it penetrates even to dividing soul and spirit, joints and marrow; it judges the thoughts and attitudes of the heart.
> -Hebrews 4:12

When we look at bringing the Bible to life for our children, why do we do it?

We do it because it offers children more than a Bible story. It offers them a place in God's Big Story. A place where they are known by God, loved by Jesus, and led by the Holy Spirit. It's a place where they are invited to be participants instead of seeing themselves as spectators.

We do it because it gives them a seat at His table no matter their age. It's where they learn that the people of the Bible are real people just like them—people with real lives full of love, dreams, victories, disappointments, and even fears.

It helps them know that God is able—and He can move in their lives. It makes space for children to be known fully as they accept the loving grace of our wonderful Savior.

When we bring the Bible to life for our kids, we can embrace the hard questions, allowing curious kids to see just how big our God is and reminding us sometimes-forgetful adults of the same.

OUR KING JESUS

Jesus, who came humbly as a baby, conquered death as King, and forgives our sins as Savior—He is near to us today. He is our friend and redeemer—our rock and our salvation. He is everything we have ever needed and more than we will ever need.

He is the same yesterday, today, and forevermore. We can rely on Him in every season. And in every circumstance, He is faithful. His Word is alive and active, holding us each day.

Jesus is with us in our homes, churches, and classrooms. And more than anything, He desires relationship with each of us and the precious children in our care.

This relationship He seeks looks like relationship *in the midst of*… in the midst of culture… in the midst of joy… in the midst of hardship… you get the picture. He is with us in all things.

When we look at the world, it can seem daunting. But it's important for us to recognize that we are part of culture and influencers of it. Culture in and of itself is not bad. We shouldn't hide from it. We shouldn't shun it. But we should navigate it with the truth of Scripture, being led by God.

The world is shouting for our kids' attention—literally coming at them with information from every direction. It's important that in the midst of this, we give them the truth that will never change. The truth of Jesus.

So, *how can we really bring the Bible to life for the kids we serve?*

There are some practical things we can do to help encourage this, as we also rely on the Holy Spirit of God to do the work that only He can.

GUIDEPOSTS FOR SHARING SCRIPTURE

One place to start is by establishing guideposts for how we frame the truth of Scripture for kids.

Share individual stories from the Bible in the context of God's Big Story.

The first thing that is so important to do is to always point stories from the Bible back to the big story of what God was, and is, doing. We want kids to see the fullness of what God was doing in those stories, so they can more clearly see how He is working in their lives today.

It's important for them to know that God moved on behalf of the people in Scripture, and He is also moving on their behalf. When they can connect the faithfulness of God throughout each story, they can see that He is trustworthy and His Word is true. They can begin to see His very personal pursuit of each one of them.

It's essential that every piece of Scripture is tied to the whole of God's Word. He is the God of our yesterday, today, and tomorrow.

This can change how children read and interpret Scripture on their own and how they view God in light of their community and personhood.

Share that the hope of the gospel is in every story.

God had a plan all along—and sin doesn't get to keep the headline. The price Jesus paid for each of us was always part of the plan, and He deserves all the glory in that! God extends to us a redemptive invitation of salvation through grace in Jesus.

Kids need to understand and see the fullness of what sin leads to—death. But it's even more important for them to understand that Jesus conquered death so that they can live in freedom and that they can have life through faith in Jesus and following God's Word.

Make sure kids understand that Jesus made the way so that they can choose Him every day.

When we reference the people in these stories, show them as real people—not characters or heroes.

The children in our care need to know that the people we speak about in the Bible are people just like them! People who make mistakes. People who have big dreams. People who believe with their whole hearts. People like you and me.

And if God can use those people, and if God can use us, He can use our kids!

Share biblical language.

It's important that we help kids understand the meaning of Scripture and biblical language within context. It opens a whole new world of how they read the Bible.

It helps us stay aligned because we add nothing to God's Word and we take nothing away—allowing children to understand the fullness of what Scripture has to offer.

Help children identify who they are in Christ.

Our identity is rooted in the same way our faith is: in being confident of what we hope for in Jesus. We become who we were created to be through claiming our inheritance as image-bearing children of God.

The more we look like Jesus, the more we look like the people He made us to be. When we take pressure off kids to *be* something, *do* something, and *become* something; they can walk in their kingdom identity.

When they understand that the God who created them knows them fully, loves them relentlessly through the personhood of Jesus, and will lead them in everything by the Holy Spirit; they can own their inheritance as His children.

The pressure to be, do, and become is off. They can rest in their Savior, walking close with Him—trusting and knowing that He will lead the way.

Choose a curriculum that does all of these things.

So that you aren't on your own as you lead, it's important that you choose a curriculum that supports these ideas. Publishers such as David C Cook create curriculum so that you aren't alone in your ministry doing this significant work.

It's important that we train our volunteers and parents around these ideas as well.

Imagine the church rallying together, building a strong foundation, so that no matter where our children go in the church; they are seeing the same truths being modeled before them.

It Comes Alive When It's Personal

Another place to start bringing the Bible to life is by consistently reaffirming what God says about our children.

Kids can know what is *always* true.

- I am known by God.
- I am loved by Jesus.
- I am led by the Holy Spirit.
- I am a child of God. And my life can tell of God's wonder.

I AM KNOWN.

God, the Creator of all, knows our kids. He has always known them. He has had them in mind from the very beginning. He made each one of them in His own image, and each is His masterpiece.

Our children are known by the Creator and that means they belong. Each one of them gets to be part of His family.

When kids understand that God knows them—all of them—it reassures them that they have nothing to hide. There's nothing to run from when you are known. It's a simple statement that brings God near to our hearts. He knows us.

Psalm 139:13-14 (NASB) says:

> *For You created my innermost parts;*
> *You wove me in my mother's womb.*
> *I will give thanks to You, because*
> *I am awesomely and wonderfully made;*
> *Wonderful are Your works,*
> *And my soul knows it very well.*

I AM LOVED.

Jesus' perfect life, death, resurrection, and promised return are God's love story. Jesus came to fulfill God's promises to His children.

Through Jesus, we each can have salvation—yes, including our kids. His love for our children has no beginning and no end, and they get to love Him back. Jesus is God's love in person. Jesus is the way to God's love.

Our children are *loved* by Jesus, and they get to share His *love*, too.

When kids comprehend that they are fully known *and* fully loved, they see just how much God really loves them. That even though He knows the messy parts of them—He loves them the same. His love and His grace are really beautiful.

It gives our children the opportunity to choose God's *love* and God's *way*.

John 13:34, 35 (NASB) says:

> *I am giving you a new commandment, that you love one another; just as I have loved you, that you also love one another. By this all people will know that you are My disciples: if you have love for one another.*

I AM LED.

God gives His followers the gift of His Holy Spirit when each chooses to live for Jesus. The Holy Spirit invites us to live in God's Kingdom—now *and* not yet. When our kids let the Holy Spirit lead, He strengthens them, and they grow in belief.

When they accept Jesus as Savior, they receive the Holy Spirit as a gift.

As our children learn that God's way is the best way, their faith grows, too. The Holy Spirit helps each one of us be more like Jesus—*the people we were made to be.*

Because our kids are *led* by the Holy Spirit, they can *follow* Him.

Romans 8:14, 15a (NASB) says:

> *For all who are being led by the Spirit of God, these are sons and daughters of God. For you have not received a spirit of slavery leading to fear again, but you have received a spirit of adoption as sons and daughters.*

As I said before, this takes the pressure off of them—the pressure to *be, do,* and *become.* They can rest in their Savior, walking close with Him—trusting and knowing that He will lead the way. This truly brings the Bible to life in a way that is almost unexplainable.

I AM A CHILD OF GOD.

God's amazing story changes our stories.

Because God knows each of us, Jesus loves us, and the Holy Spirit leads us; we each get to be a wonder-filled reflection of God to the world. Our children get to know who they truly are and who they were made to be. God delights in them!

The Bible tells our children that they are fearfully and wonderfully made, knit together by a loving God who knows all about them and loves every bit of them.

Our children are *wonders*. They get to *be* part of God's story, and their lives *tell* of God's wonder.

1 Peter 2:9 (NASB) says:

> *But you are a chosen people, a royal priesthood, a holy nation, a people for God's own possession, so that you may proclaim the excellencies of Him who has called you out of darkness into His marvelous light.*

MAKING SPACE FOR RESPONSE

I don't know about you, but when I understand the degree to which someone knows me and loves me, I tend to respond differently to them. If I know that someone doesn't have my best interest at heart, I am less likely to listen to and follow their advice or thoughts toward me.

When my parents or my husband shares something with me, I am more apt to listen and to respond. I listen because I know the level of care they have for me.

It's the same way with God. When we paint a picture of an impersonal God who serves the world at a distance, our children are less likely to respond to His Word and what He's called each of us to.

But when they know that He fully sees them, knows them, hears them, and loves them; they realize they can trust Him with *everything*. It's so important that we make space within our ministries for children to respond to God—whether through song, writing, drawing, creating, painting, praying, or something else!

And of course, as with anything, we can make it sound simple. But simple language can really bring to light the most complex things in the world.

In 1 Corinthians 1:26-31 (NASB), Scripture says:

> *For consider your calling, brothers and sisters, that there were not many wise according to the flesh, not many mighty, not many noble; but God has chosen the foolish things of the world to shame the wise, and God has chosen the weak things of the world to shame the things which are strong, and the insignificant things of the world and the despised God has chosen, the things that are not, so that He may nullify the things that are, so that no human may boast before God. But it is due to Him that you are in Christ Jesus, who became to us wisdom from God, and righteousness and sanctification, and redemption, so that, just as it is written: "Let the one who boasts, boast in the Lord."*

With God moving, our children can know that His Word is alive and active. That His commands are true. That He is near to them and is with them—no matter what the cultural context says and no matter what it looks like in the future. His Word remains steadfast and true.

Make space in your ministry for children to respond to the God who knows them, loves them, leads them. Make space for them to understand their identity as His kids.

IN THE MIDST OF THE WORLD

Beth Guckenberger, who some of you may know (and love!), was speaking once at David C Cook. She was speaking to a group of women when she brought up Caesarea Philippi and Matthew 16:13-20.

Now, I'm not going to say this as well as she did, but I'm hoping you'll catch the main point here in my cliff-notes version.

The people of Caesarea Philippi worshipped gods of the underworld (fertility gods, specifically, Pan) and had major sexual perversion. Also, in Caesarea Philippi, there was a cliff with a hole that they believed the gods traveled through like a 'gate from Hell.' It was a whole thing. I encourage you to look it up!

Caesarea Philippi was miles outside of where Jesus would normally teach, so it feels very intentional that He went there.

And in Matthew 16:18-19 (NASB), this is where Jesus was when He said, *"Upon this rock I will build My church; and the gates of Hades will not overpower it. I will give you the keys of the kingdom of heaven; and whatever you bind on earth shall have been bound in heaven, and whatever you loose on earth shall have been loosed in heaven."*

Woah.

I wrote earlier about how Jesus offers us a relationship in the midst of. Here He addresses how He will build His Church. We all know that He is the Cornerstone—the foundation. But could He have been saying more?

Could He have been saying that He was going to build His Church *in the midst of*?

In the midst of the world, a world full of sexual perversion, in a city that didn't welcome Him. And guess what! The gates of hell would not prevail. He is going to build His Church right next to the gates of hell, and they won't stand a chance.

In all of the discouragement we could experience as we look out at the world today, we have to remember that when we serve Jesus and give Him our kids, we are part of this Church. The one that the gates of hell will not win against.

This is why we need to do our best to introduce our kids in our ministries to Jesus. The one who knows them and loves them and leads them. As they come to know Him, they will learn to trust Him. Because when they are with Him, He is with them—in the midst of anything that may come their way.

He wins. Jesus always wins. And He shows up in the most unlikely (and sure) places to remind us of who He is.

TIME FOR REFLECTION

As we work to bring the Bible to life for kids, here are some questions to think through.

At the beginning of this chapter, I addressed the why. *Why do we do what we do to bring Scripture to life?* Let me remind you of that.

We do it because it offers children more than a Bible story. It offers them a place in God's Big Story. A place where they are known by God, loved by Jesus, and led by the Holy Spirit. It's a place where they are invited to be participants instead of seeing themselves as spectators.

We do it because it gives them a seat at His table no matter their age. It's where they learn that the people of the Bible are real people just like them—people with real lives full of love, dreams, victories, disappointments, and even fears.

It helps them know that God is able—and He can move in their lives. It makes space for children to be known fully as they accept the loving grace of our wonderful Savior.

When we bring the Bible to life for our kids, we can embrace the hard questions, allowing curious kids to see just how big our God is and reminding us sometimes-forgetful adults of the same.

No matter where culture turns next, we have a constant, true, and faithful King whose words breathe truth in the most unlikely (and sure) places. He is reliable and we can trust our children with Him.

His name is Jesus. [period]

| LIVING IT OUT |

- *Am I intentional about making space for Jesus to be King of my ministry? What are some things I can do differently so I can do this even better? Am I giving children the language they need?*

- *How am I making space for the living Word of God to move? Do my plans and responses allow God to work in the ways He intends, or do my intentions and opinions get in the way?*

- *How am I making space for curiosity and questions within my ministry? Do the kids, parents, and volunteers in my ministry feel safe to ask the hard things?*

JESUS FOR ALL
SPECIAL NEEDS

Stephen "Doc" Hunsley, M.D.

> Jesus answered, "It was neither that this man sinned, nor his parents; but it was so that the works of God might be displayed in him."
> -John 9:3

What Would Jesus Do? That is easy! Jesus would do Special Needs Ministry! Look at Jesus' time on earth; 75% of His recorded miracles were on those with disabilities. He healed the lame, blind, deaf, mute, and so on. Jesus was the first Special Needs Pastor!

In John 9, Jesus healed a man who had been blind since birth. His disciples asked Him who caused this – the sin of the man or his parents. I love Jesus' answer in vs 3: *"Jesus answered, 'It was neither that this man sinned, nor his parents; but it was so that the works of God might be displayed in him.'"*

Every individual with a disability is created in the image and likeness of God! They are created on purpose and for a purpose! They are not a mistake! Our mistake is being "afraid" of their diagnosis and not knowing what to do, so we put our heads in the sand and don't welcome them into our ministry. This is NOT what Jesus wants!

Luke 14 is the parable of the wedding feast, and Jesus uses this parable as a command for churches AND your kidmin to welcome individuals with special needs. The wedding feast represents the Church and there were more seats available, Jesus told them in verses 13-14: *"But whenever you give a banquet, invite people who are poor, who have disabilities, who are limping, and people who are blind; 14 and you will be blessed."* Jesus uses this parable as a command for the church and every kidmin to welcome those with disabilities into their church. Why? Because the church and your kidmin need those with disabilities just as much as those with disabilities need your church and kidmin! This is so important that Jesus followed this up immediately with another parable of a wedding feast and in verse 21, shares the exact command again – except He says to "Go out at once" to find our friends! Plus, don't miss one of the amazing promises in this passage! If you do this, your ministry will be **blessed**! I, along with SOAR Special Needs, have now assisted over 500 churches in starting a Special Needs Ministry throughout the United States and 12 Countries around the World, and I can attest that every one of those has truly been blessed by Jesus!

Person-first language – Individuals with special needs first and foremost are a person, not a disability. Therefore, the most appropriate way to refer to a person with disabilities is by placing the focus on the person first, before you name the disability. An example is: "a boy with autism" or a "teen with Down syndrome" rather than "an autistic boy" or "a Down's teen."

Special Needs Ministry is no longer an elective for kidmin, it is now a requirement! This doesn't mean you need to have a full Special Needs Ministry, but it DOES mean that you need to be able to accept individuals with disabilities into your kidmin and not turn them away.

You might be saying right now, "We don't have anyone with special needs in our kidmin." I would like to challenge you on that. Many parents are not willing to tell you that their child may be on the autism spectrum because they are afraid that they might be asked to leave your church! Families with disabilities are asked weekly to leave their church all across the country. Not only that, but the latest statistics show that one out of every six children have a disability in the US. (New number reportedly will be 1 in 4 by late 2022!) If you have a kidmin of more than six children, you most likely have an individual with special needs! Some children may be currently undiagnosed but receive a diagnosis in the future – their disability, whether officially diagnosed or not, still impacts their church experience. Statistically, for every person you've seen who looks disabled, you've seen at least 4 more individuals who are disabled but don't look it. Hidden disabilities include Traumatic Brain Injury, Epilepsy, ADD, Learning Disabilities, and Mental Health like major depression, bipolar disorder, schizophrenia and anxiety disorders, post-traumatic stress disorder, etc.

Families with disabilities are also one of the largest unmet people groups in the US! It is estimated that 90% of families with disabilities do not attend church. At the same time, according to a study by Erik Carter (2016), only 11% of all evangelical churches today are offering programming for individuals with special needs! This is not what Jesus would do! That means that 89% of churches today are not welcoming to families with individuals with special needs! This is a huge opportunity for outreach and discipleship. It is also a way for the church to make positive inroads in a community and say "we see you, the disability community, and we value you!"

The vast majority of kidmin I've met want their ministry to reach people in their community and grow. If the percentage of children with special needs in your local school system doesn't compare to the percentage of children with special needs in your kidmin, you need to ask yourself why! Where is the disconnect when it comes to families with disabilities? If you, as a kidmin leader haven't experienced disability through a friend or family member, then you might not realize that special needs affect every community; all ethnicities, all ages, and all social classes. Start asking what you need to do to engage this population in your community; every church can start somewhere.

A disability—no matter what kind, or what severity—does not make anyone less of a human being. Every living, breathing person has a spirit that is capable of responding to the Holy Spirit. Never assume that anyone is beyond the ability of God to touch their lives in some significant way. The work of the Holy Spirit is not limited by one's disabling condition. Jesus died for all equally, not just those without disabilities.

What does a Special Needs Ministry look like? It is different for every church and kidmin! You have to find what is right for your ministry. But it starts with welcoming those you already have and becoming inclusive with them! The definition of special needs in regards to ministry and the church:

- Any need a family member may have that requires some forethought to ensure that the family's church experience is meaningful and safe. This includes severe allergies, medical issues, or cognitive differences.
- A special needs ministry is a ministry to the ENTIRE family, not just the individual with special needs!

Special Needs Ministry exists to impart the Word of God in the heart of all individuals engagingly and understandably and to teach them to love, know, and honor God. The **church needs to be a place of refuge for families with special needs** where the parents know that their child is loved on and showered with the love of Jesus! An Inclusive Church means that we want all of our individuals with special needs to feel that they are valued and as important as every other individual that comes into your church. Inclusive classrooms are places where all students are VITAL members of the classroom, feel a connection to their peers, and have access to a meaningful 'general' education curriculum, but may need to receive support to succeed. It also means that **no one ever ages out of your special needs programming!** That elementary-age child will eventually be a high schooler and then an adult, and if you don't have programming for them, you are telling the family that your church doesn't welcome them.

3 GOALS OF A SPECIAL NEEDS MINISTRY – FOR A CHURCH:

1. Open the door to share the Gospel with families affected by special needs and introduce them to a personal relationship with God
2. Integrate those with disabilities into the life of the church and give them opportunities to actively serve God
3. Enable the church to serve as a witness to the community by meeting the spiritual, physical, and social needs of families affected by special needs.

5 SPECIFIC GOALS OF A SPECIAL NEEDS MINISTRY – FOR THE MINISTRY

1. To integrate students into an age/developmentally appropriate classroom
2. To make all feel welcomed and loved within their class
3. To provide buddies to students/adults who need assistance
4. To allow each student/adult to feel God's love through their buddy
5. To share Christ's love

So now it is your turn to make a difference! Making your kidmin inclusive doesn't have to be something scary. There are several simple steps that everyone can start with!

First, **pray** and ask God what His desire is for your kidmin. Pray that God will provide the leadership, volunteers, and resources necessary to meet the needs. This will produce a whole new group of volunteers who are not even engaged in serving in your church yet!

Next, **start small** - start with what you already have! You don't need to have a full program, just be willing to start. This can begin by simply getting a buddy (one-on-one "peer") for a child with disabilities so they can be included in their age-appropriate or developmentally appropriate classroom. The buddy can be an adult or a teenager who is paired with the individual with disabilities so that they would be able to participate to their full potential. I do not recommend that you use parents or siblings as buddies. They need to be able to attend their own worship to get their spiritual gas tanks filled, and we want our individuals with disabilities to have as many relationships as possible. Parents are advocating and working for their children every day of the week. Let's help make Sunday a true Sabbath for these families!

What is the role of a buddy?
1. Share the love of Jesus with your individual
2. Ensure the safety of the individual
3. Be a guide on the side
4. Allow for independence when appropriate
5. Help the individual get the most out of the teacher-generated curriculum
6. Encourage your individual to interact with their peers and others around them
7. Focus on their abilities, not disabilities
8. Be positive – especially when talking with parents
9. Never be isolated 1:1 alone
10. Know techniques to encourage success

Volunteers often feel unqualified, but the only requirement they need is answering: can they be a friend? That is really what they will be. You can train and prepare them for everything else! Of course, you will still follow background checks and all other guidelines you have for your other kidmin volunteers. The basis of this ministry needs to be relational!

The third step is to designate a Special Needs Ministry Champion – this person helps form the vision and is the major cheerleader for the ministry – THIS MIGHT BE YOU! This person doesn't need to be on staff, they can be a volunteer, and could even be a parent. Following this, you will build a leadership team. At first, it may only be 2-3 people. They share the vision and passion and help determine the ministry's strategies and promote the ministry's vision. From here, you can now focus on building the ministry team. Share the vision and stories of how this ministry impacts families and volunteer to get volunteers and leaders to join you. Make it personal! Make direct asks through shoulder tapping – because bulletins don't typically work!

Casting vision is CRUCIAL! Why do you need volunteers? "SOAR exists to transform the lives of special families and empower them to SOAR in their local and faith communities." By providing buddies for individuals with special needs, we can better help them engage with the lessons and come to know Jesus! Be passionate when sharing volunteer opportunities. Empowering people to volunteer is all about helping them imagine their ability to fill a role. We need to switch to story-based versus need-based recruitment. Millennials especially want to be a part of things that create change, not to "fill holes." Remove "filling holes" from your vocabulary – this mindset is a temporary fix and does not have a people-focused mindset! Share stories of life change and belonging when discussing your ministry with future volunteers.

When it comes to recruiting volunteers for your ministry, the four most important letters of the alphabet are I.C.N.U. Actively observe other people in your church for characteristics that would make

effective volunteers or leaders in your area and then share with them…
I see in you (I.C.N.U.) someone who has a gift of… (your observations about their giftset) and then ask them "Can you be a friend?" This is the heart of what it takes to be a buddy. Let them know you can provide all the other information they need, and assure them that they don't need any experience. Then ask them to pray about serving with you and talk with them in a week or two about it. This is the most effective way to get volunteers, and these are the ones who stick with it and stay for the long haul! Plus, you let God do all of the heavy lifting for you! I have a 90-95% success rate using this model! Examples of this include:

- "I see in you (I.C.N.U.)…."
- "I think you would be great at …."
- "Can you be a friend?"
- "Would you be willing to pray about serving as a …. and talk more about what that might look like in a week or two?"
- Focus on their skills, giftsets, and how they are already equipped.

PRAY! PRAY! PRAY! Pick a time every day for your entire team to pray together for your ministry, your volunteers, and your families. Pick huge God-sized goals to pray for and pray through those to allow God to answer those prayers!

Recruit the youth ministry – they can be your best and most faithful volunteers – offer community service hours! Partner with a local university; students are pursuing degrees in special education, early childhood education, or family ministry. Partner with local high school groups and organizations: National Honor Society, leadership groups, sports teams, etc. are often looking for community service hour opportunities. This is also a great form of evangelism! I have led many volunteers to Christ because they served as a buddy (where they don't do the teaching and don't need to have a faith story, but are willing to be a friend and serve)! It only takes a few weeks and their eyes and heart are open for you to share Jesus with them!

Ministry visibility is also important as having participants of the ministry serve in the church increases the ministry's awareness. Encourage volunteers to recruit their friends to serve with them! Watch whom your participants approach at church and invite them to join your ministry. They recognize who has a heart for those with special needs!

All volunteers should go through an application, background check (if over 18 y/o), and training before serving. Safety and security are a MUST for your ministry! More on this in a minute.

Scout current volunteers for passion and commitment to your vision and engagement in their walk with God. It is WAY easier to grow someone's skill level than their commitment level. Skill improvement is equipping with more knowledge and experience (external factors), but commitment is only grown internally. Look for volunteers who have been brought in over time (a few months at least), not new volunteers – you must determine if this enthusiasm is because it's a new and exciting role – plus it helps them to learn the D.N.A. of your ministry and to fully embrace your vision.

Recruit leaders because of their gifts and passions, not because of your ministry's needs. SOAR's Volunteer Encouragement leader was recruited out of a passion for encouraging others, not because we initially recognized it was an area that could be volunteer-led. This is also a HUGE way for God to grow your ministry, as others have convictions and passions for this community that might complement your own or expand your ministry reach. Do you have a specific role you need to fill? Look for someone who is bought into that aspect of your ministry; don't try to force a talented volunteer into being passionate about it. This may take time, but be patient. It is easier to wait than to train several volunteers that don't stick.

Recruit your replacement! What should be your weekly goal? Make yourself unnecessary - frees you up to encourage volunteers, welcome families, or jump into a role if someone cancels. Also, it allows the ministry to go on without you at the same quality if you suddenly are unavailable. It also equips other leaders to do special needs ministry full-time. Some churches have a passion for planting churches/campuses, but it's also good to equip leaders to help other churches start ministries of their own.

Welcoming those individuals with disabilities that are already in your church and letting them feel a part of your kidmin is the next big step. This goes beyond just saying hi to the individual with special needs. A disability ministry needs to minister to the entire family. Talk with the family and see how they are doing. Let them know you are praying for them. When you have new families visit your kidmin and you learn that they have an individual with special needs, your first question is NOT "what do I need to know?!" Your first question to the family needs to be: **"Tell me something wonderful about (child's name)?"** Many times, the parents will start telling you about the diagnosis and the problems. Kindly stop them and say, no, first I want to hear what is wonderful about them. Most likely, you will start to see tears because no one has ever asked these parents that before! Everyone just wants to know what the potential problems are and how to deal with them. Learn to focus on an individual's abilities, not their disabilities.

Be sure to address an individual with special needs directly, not just talking with their parent or caregiver. Even if they are nonverbal, they are still present in the conversation and need to be included.

Creating a welcoming environment also includes the realization that many children with disabilities have sensory issues and may not be able to tolerate the bright lights or the loud noise that we frequently have in kidmin. You can simply prepare for this by offering headphones or disposable earplugs to help offset the noise, and cheap sunglasses can help with the lighting. This is a powerful way to communicate to families "you are known, loved, and valued in our church" and "we want to worship WITH you!" These individuals may also have times that they are disruptive or loud during your service. Teach your volunteers and others that their presence is more important than having a perfect service. Realize that everyone worships differently and learn to welcome the diversity that you have created by allowing every person to worship.

3 Steps to Supporting Individuals with Special Needs:

1. **Plan to include:** modify the work of the student so they can be included with the other students and if they need assistance give it to them.
2. **Ask and listen:** ask the individual/parent what kind of support that student needs. This allows the student and parents to feel respected as it's better to ask than assume!!
3. **Step back:** allow the students to be independent when they can, and allow them to do activities with their peers.

Next, train your volunteers. I believe you need to train ALL of your kidmin volunteers, not just those who will be buddies. Many children today are undiagnosed and in the classroom. Your kidmin teachers and volunteers will need to know how to handle any behaviors that might occur. You can ask special education teachers in your church for assistance on this. You can also reach out to a Disability Organization that can assist you with training and planning your ministry – this is one of the specialties of SOAR Special Needs! We are happy to assist you by providing training, coaching, or consulting. Check us out at SOARSpecialNeeds.org or info@SOARSpecialNeeds.org! By using training to teach learning techniques to help children with disabilities, you strengthen your kidmin program and help your volunteers and leaders become better equipped to serve your families.

It's not enough to help a volunteer see they are capable of being a part of your ministry; you also need to give them the tools to succeed with the individuals they are working with. Through training, your volunteers learn to be successful rather than fearful. Also, remember that training is not accomplished all at once. Training is best when you offer additional opportunities to build skills and coach volunteers along the way. Help people realize that they do not need experience with special needs, just a heart to serve! Remember the question, "Can you be a friend?" Use case scenarios for training. This allows volunteers to learn by working through real weekend experiences. Use this training for all new volunteers. You DON'T have to create this! SOAR already has a ninety-minute case-based scenario training that allows volunteers to learn principles and policies in the first half, then apply their knowledge through scenario discussions. If you want some examples of this, reach out to SOAR or check out our YouTube: SOARSpecialNeeds.

Proper use of affection:
- Many individuals with special needs love to show affection with hugs, kissing, and sitting on your lap.
- Buddies should only give side hugs, high-fives, and fist bumps.
- Do not allow kissing, no frontal hugs, and no lap sitting.

Allow new volunteers an opportunity to shadow experienced volunteers before serving on their own. Ensure the volunteer that they are shadowing knows they are there to follow them, encourage them to ask questions, and engage with the participant. This is a helpful way to gauge future leaders; watch them build up new volunteers!

Offer higher-level training for committed volunteers. Nonviolent Crisis Intervention training by C.P.I. is expensive but helpful (contact SOAR about cost-effective ways!) For SOAR, this training (with holds) is required for leaders/coordinators, and the de-escalation techniques are highly encouraged for all volunteers who have served for six months or longer.

Gracefully correct and improve volunteer techniques. Watch volunteers interact with their participants and offer feedback. Reinforce good interactions; point out good interventions and interactions whenever possible. When correcting a technique, use a sandwich approach. Point out a way they do their job well, offer the correction, then express another way they do what they do well. Typically, it is unhelpful to correct mid-behavior, but the sooner, the better. Don't correct a technique that was used weeks after it occurred. You have now lost that opportunity to teach. Encourage feedback from the volunteers if in an inclusive setting, but encourage them to call you mid-behavior next time if there is a concern with how it's being dealt with. It is easier to work with a buddy when you see the interaction yourself.

Quarterly buddy gathering is an opportunity to grow skills four times a year. NEVER call these training events because NO ONE will come for extra training! However, if you call it a buddy gathering or a social, everyone will come out for the community! This is a dual-purpose event; focuses on improving skills, while also encouraging community. This all prevents vision leak! It is vital to be discussing ministry values, incorporate worship into the session, pray for one another, encourage fun, and have an opportunity to be outward-focused. You remind volunteers of the purpose of the ministry and teach an important topic that they may need to learn about. For instance, how to work with an individual who is non-verbal would be good. Use the games/social aspects as a tie-in to the lesson itself. For non-verbal communication, you can use the telephone game but non-verbally! Some other ideas could be to train on limit setting – play three rounds of a game, one without rules/limits, one with too many, and one with a good balance. Then discuss that and the importance of having enforceable limits. You don't need a big budget/any budget to do these events successfully. Do it between meal times, offer a Christmas cookie exchange, or find inexpensive/free games to play.

You can also offer your volunteers opportunities for a response, like buddy assessments. These are a half sheet asking about the good, bad, and ugly of the service. It creates an opportunity for follow-up during the week, encouraging volunteers who had a hard service and helping them grow their skills. It is also helpful in tracking participant behavior shifts, as well as knowing what's going on in the lives of your volunteers. The most important element of these assessments is the prayer question. We pray weekly for volunteers by name who fill this out!

Now it is time to engage church leadership. When ministry leaders understand and support the vision of your program, it is more likely to thrive. It tends to flourish when pastors see the value and become actively involved in a special needs ministry. Get your church leadership on your team. Promote your ministry to your congregation and your fellow staff members. The families that you serve are a vital part of the body of Christ. Keep them and your ministry in front of people all the time. You and your church leadership are on the same side of the battle to advance the kingdom of God. Our role is to call each other to greater commitment levels in that battle; not to fight against one another. Serve your leaders by providing them with helpful and accurate information on a variety of topics over time (i.e., over-stimulation). This requires an ongoing process. Your church leadership and congregation will likely rely on you to provide them with continuing education as a step in transforming your church into a welcoming place for people with disabilities and their families. Offer it to them at a pace that they can handle. With a sense of perspective, disability ministry is not the only ministry of the church that is attempting to educate the congregation and its leaders.

Network with other churches already doing special needs ministry. The SOAR Disability Ministry Network meets over zoom monthly with special needs ministry leaders from all over the world where you can learn from others, ask questions, and share resources! Sign up for the next one at SOARSpecialNeeds.org/Events.

How do you partner with your families? Make them part of your vision and meet them where they are at. Create programs that meet their needs, not your dreams. The most important thing to remember is to ask yourself, "What would I want if I were the parent?"

When working with individuals with special needs, we need to remember that their brain does not allow them to transition from one thing to another quickly. It takes time and a lot of prepping! There are several things you can do as a ministry to help with this. First, consider visual schedules. They use images, symbols, or photos to better communicate an activity or task to your friend. Using your own pictures of your actual environments helps them to focus and carry out tasks or transition between activities. This works wonderfully for verbal and non-verbal individuals. Visual Timers are also extremely helpful with the transition, but now they can watch the time click down, and see how long before they need to transition to the next task. Social stories are an easy and effective way of teaching individuals with special needs by using visual and or written cues to help them navigate through unfamiliar social situations. This is written in first person and for the appropriate developmental skill level using pictures.

If you have the room or budget, a Sensory Space can be very valuable. It is an environment where individuals who need a break from typical sensory input, or who need sensory input not found in a typical classroom, can have their sensory needs met so that they can continue to learn about Jesus. A sensory space could be any of the following:

- A bag/box in a classroom
- A corner in a classroom with a tent/chair
- A board (even portable) that can be in a classroom or a hall
- A sensory room – a room dedicated just for sensory space for special needs.

Items for a sensory space:

- Cognitive toys - cause & effect toys (musical toys, computers), puzzles, etc.
- Sensory toys - massagers, koosh balls, light-up toys, etc.
- Fine motor toys- puzzles, blocks, Legos, etc.
- Things for vestibular and proprioception input - swings, trampolines, rocking chair
- Things for social interaction - toys that take two or more people to play, games, etc.
- Fidgets - tangle toys, water-filled balls, rainsticks, etc. (McDonald's Happy Meal toys work great and parents are happy to donate them!)
- Miscellaneous – headphones, earplugs, timers, adaptive scissors, body sock, giant pea pod, fluorescent light covers, etc.

Check out www.SpecialNeedsToys.com

Engage learning tools to help teach your lessons. Try to start including auditory, visual, and hands-on learning tools in your classrooms. Be willing to take risks and try new things to include everyone. If it doesn't work, simply move on to the next idea. The important thing to remember is that you are trying to include and welcome everyone for who they are and where they are. This doesn't mean changing your entire kidmin. It can be as simple as teaching the Bible verse for the week in sign language to help include your individuals who might be non-verbal. We can change how the lesson is delivered without changing the message of Jesus!

Every church is different and every special needs ministry is different. However, one thing is the same! Jesus. [period] My prayer is that you will evaluate your kidmin program and see how you can start welcoming families with disabilities into what you already do each week! Don't be afraid, just be willing to be a friend and share Jesus with these amazing friends! You will be amazed how God blesses your ministry! SOAR Special Needs is here to help you! Come SOAR with us!

Jesus must be our example in everything we do! We already learned that Jesus was the first Special Needs Pastor and He used John 9 and Luke 14 to call every church and kidmin to welcome individuals with special needs! Jesus is for all: Special Needs. [period] Now let's do our part and just be like Jesus. [period]

[LIVING IT OUT]

- *How effective are you in reaching individuals with special needs in your kidmin?*

- *What are your first steps in following John 9 and Luke 14 to welcome kids with special needs into your ministry? Don't forget about SOAR Special Needs!*

- *How are you going to get the rest of your staff on board to support a special needs ministry?*

JESUS FOCUSED
THE CENTER OF YOUR THOUGHTS

Debbie Rhoads

> Finally, brothers and sisters, whatever is true, whatever
> is noble, whatever is right, whatever is pure, whatever is
> lovely, whatever is admirable—if anything is excellent or
> praiseworthy—think about such things. Whatever you have
> learned or received or heard from me, or seen in me—put it
> into practice. And the God of peace will be with you.
> -Philippians 4:8-9

I truly believe that children's ministry leaders are among the most creative people on the planet. Who else can decorate an entire church for VBS with pool noodles, cardboard boxes, and empty toilet paper rolls… and make it look amazing? Who else can captivate children and teach them about God's love and awesomeness with yarn, a rubber chicken, a plunger, and a few balloons? We are a creative people. However, our creativity doesn't stop there, at least not for me. I have an incredible ability to create scenarios in my mind. Maybe you share in this "gift/curse."

I'm not just talking about beautiful, pleasant scenarios of kid's classrooms full of prepared volunteers and perfectly behaved children. I'm talking about creating scenarios full of "what if's," "why did they do that," "what were they thinking," and "they must think that about me."

Can anyone relate?

A text message comes in from the Pastor. It's short, to the point, and somewhat abrupt. You read the text and your mind wanders, "He must be upset with me about something. Why did he say it like that? Did I do something wrong? It must be because I spoke up in the meeting. I thought he received my feedback well? I guess, not. Is he questioning my leadership? Should I schedule a meeting to talk to him?"

Whew!

The reality is that the Pastor was at his son's soccer game and only had a quick second to respond but didn't want to wait any longer to respond out of respect for your time, so he shot over a quick, to the point response. Done.

Well, that was embarrassing.

Or how about this one? One of your volunteers took initiative and prepped the lesson supplies for Sunday and set up the classrooms. They had never done that before and you were very surprised. Before you know it, your mind goes into overdrive. "Why did she do that? Doesn't she know I like things done a certain way? Is what I do not good enough? She must want my job. That's it! She doesn't like me and she's trying to show me up. She thinks she can do this better than me. I wonder if she is trying to turn people against me."

The reality is she saw how much was on your plate and had some extra time. She wanted to bless you and surprise you. She knew it wasn't exactly the way you normally do it, but she tried her best. She loves what you do and how you lead and wanted to let you know that you are supported and loved.

Yikes! Once again, that was embarrassing! Thank God no one knew what was going on inside your head. Yes, these examples are quite extreme. However, the point is that our mind has a way of taking over and wreaking havoc. This havoc takes away our peace.

Jesus is peace. If we have Jesus in the center of our ministry, we will be at peace. When our spirit is not at peace, you will know that something else is in the center of your ministry... and it's not Jesus. Let's be real, many times we are the cause of our lack of peace. Our creative minds, that is.

In today's world, our minds are inundated with stuff... so much stuff. The internet, emails, social media, texts, meetings, the news. Not to mention the overwhelming number of streaming services available. The outlets in which communication is pushed out are endless. No wonder we are challenged when it comes to our thoughts.

We teach our kids to be careful what we put into our minds. We sing songs like "Oh, be careful little minds what you think..." However, as adults, we often forget these simple basics that will protect us. The enemy would like nothing more than to have us second guess ourselves, to create "thought bubbles" over people's head, to not trust those we are serving with or who we are ministering to. He would rather our minds be in turmoil because he knows that what we speak is from the heart, and what is in our heart comes from our thoughts (Matthew 15:18-19).

Let's imagine for a moment what it would be like if Jesus was at the center of our thoughts. Just Jesus. We would assume the best in everyone. We would be positive. We would be realistic. We would give people the benefit of the doubt. We would have more time because we wouldn't be wasting it on creating things that were not true. We wouldn't second guess ourselves. We would be confident in who are in Christ. We would be at peace. What an amazing concept for our ministry.

The good news is, we can control what we think about. WE get to choose what goes into our mind, what gets to stay, and what must go. We can have a ministry where Jesus is the center of our thoughts. Here are some practical tips to make this a reality.

Don't assume. If you don't have full understanding about something, ask questions and get clarity. Asking questions doesn't make you weak. Rather, it shows that you value the person and relationship. Assuming can get us into trouble. It leaves things open to our own interpretation. This can specifically be detrimental when you are forming relationships and you do not know the person very well.

Communicate in person as much as possible. In today's culture, it's very easy to hide behind a text message, an email, or even a phone call. There is something to be said for face-to-face interaction. Being able to see a person's facial expressions and their body language often speaks louder than their words. It allows you to see the true heart behind what they are trying to say.

I make it a rule on my team that we do not have difficult conversations over email and certainly not text. Occasionally, due to logistics, we may have to converse over the phone, however, this is a rare occurrence. Even basic conversations over text/email can get a little derailed, if not careful.

Example: Sue had some family issues arise and can't come into work. Of course, she isn't going to see you in person so the next best thing would be to call you on the phone. However, Sue decides to send a text message telling you that she's not coming in, but she will make up her hours later in the week. You are in back-to-back meetings, and you don't want to forget to respond so you quickly send back your response of, "Fine."

You are totally fine with Sue taking care of her family issues and making up her time later. However, Sue can't see your heart and understanding in your response of "fine." You have left much for interpretation. Sue's thoughts are now all over the place. "Are you really "fine," or are you saying "fine" like you are mad?" "Does she need to just come in?" "Is her job in jeopardy?" We could go on and on. The point is, communicate well. Leave little room for wayward interpretations.

Fill your mind with good things. This goes back to the kid's song we sang earlier. Yes, we have a lot of information coming at us. However, we do have control of what we listen to.

I have a friend who was obsessed with watching/listening to the news. I'm not saying there is anything wrong with this. Being informed is important. However, there were new stations playing in her home 24 hours a day. It was in the background as she cleaned. She watched it when she drank her morning coffee. It was on over dinner. She went to sleep to it and woke up to it. I knew the news was a big part of my friend's life, however, I didn't realize the extent until I stayed at her home one weekend. Within a few hours of being in her home with the news stations playing non-stop, I found myself feeling very anxious. After the first full day, I was completely overwhelmed. No wonder why my friend struggled with peace in her life. Her mind had no room for anything but what the news stations filled it with.

I felt like I needed to say something to my friend. She honesty never saw the correlation but thought it made sense. She limited her news consumption to an hour a day and turned on worship music for the rest of the time. Her anxiety began to fade as it was replaced with peace. What goes into your mind really does make a difference.

Use Philippians 4:8-9 as a filter. God gave us the ability to choose our thoughts. However, He knew we would sometimes struggle with it. I believe that is why He had Paul give us instructions in the Bible. Paul writes to us out of experience, and I paraphrase, "if you want peace, you can only think of these things…"

This may seem trivial and even a bit silly, but I promise you, this works. The more you practice this, the easier it gets. When you have a thought, run it through the filter of *"Fix your thoughts on what is true, and honorable, and right, and pure, and lovely, and admirable. Think about things that are excellent and worthy of praise."* If your thoughts are not these things, then you must NOT think about it.

A thought starts looming through your mind:

- **Is it true?** It needs to be real and not false. If it's not true, STOP! YOU CAN'T THINK ABOUT IT.
- **Is it honorable?** If it's not dignified, of high regard and brings glory to God, STOP! YOU CAN'T THINK ABOUT IT.
- **Is it right?** Your thought should be just, proper, and not mistaken. If it is not right, STOP! YOU CAN'T THINK ABOUT IT.
- **Is it pure?** It needs to be without spot and unadulterated. If it's not pure, STOP! YOU CAN'T THINK ABOUT IT.
- **Is it lovely?** If it's not beautiful and sweet, STOP! YOU CAN'T THINK ABOUT IT.
- **Is it admirable?** Your thoughts should bring high esteem and be worthy of admiration. If they do not, STOP! YOU CAN'T THINK ABOUT IT.
- **Is it excellent?** It needs to be of great worth. If it's not excellent, STOP! YOU CAN'T THINK ABOUT IT.
- **Is it worthy of praise?** If it is not worthy to be applauded and would not be approved by God, STOP! YOU CAN'T THINK ABOUT IT.

Before you know it, your mind has Jesus at the center of all your thoughts. You are at peace, even when things get a little crazy in life. Peace.

Take your thoughts captive. Remember that YOU get to choose what thoughts can stay, and what thoughts must flee. In II Corinthians 10:3-5 we are told that we must make every thought obedient to Christ. Meaning, if it doesn't go through the above filter, get rid of it! Do not entertain it. Do not allow it take up residence. Do not even let it visit. Your peace depends on it.

Your thoughts rarely stay just thoughts. They affect your very being and pour out of your heart and affect your ministry and those around you. Your ministry can be taken to the next level or completely destroyed… by your thoughts. The choice is up to you. Allow the center of your thoughts to be Jesus. [period]

[LIVING IT OUT]

- *What are some of the ways your thoughts have gotten in the way of peace in your ministry?*

- *Which filter(s) from Philippians 4:8-9 do your thoughts usually get caught up in?*

- *Starting today, what can you do to put Jesus back in the center of your though*

JESUS FOLLOWERS FOR LIFE

RESILIENT DISCIPLES

The KidzMatter Team

> To the Jews who had believed him, Jesus said,
> "If you hold to my teaching, you are really my disciples.
> Then you will know the truth,
> and the truth will set you free."
> -John 8:31-32

Why do you do what you do? What is your why for serving in ministry? We've already asked you this question, but truly stop for a moment and think. Think back to when God called you into kidmin. Reflect on that why for a few moments. (We will wait!)

Obviously, if you are reading this book, you agree that children's ministry is awesome! (Where else can shaving cream fights and toilet paper cannons be considered work, right?) But you didn't start working in kidmin just for unlimited goldfish and juice boxes. You didn't start serving because you love cleaning up glitter spills and changing diapers. For many of you, you probably didn't start serving just because you like working with kids, either.

You've heard us say it before, but hear us again. What you do matters! Your actions on a Sunday morning can make an eternal difference in the life of a boy or girl. This… this is why you do you what you do. This is why you give up vacation days and family time. Every sacrifice, every exhausting day… it's all worth it.

We have the best job on the planet because we get to teach boys and girls the love of Jesus.

If that's the why for serving, what is the goal? What do you spend time planning and prepping for? By the time boys and girls leave your area of ministry what do you hope is accomplished? (Take another few moments and think on this if you need.)

Our Operations Director, Amber Pike, shares this story about her first summer teaching at VBS as a teen.

> The year I turned 16, I was finally old enough to be an assistant teaching in VBS instead of just a helper. Man, was I excited. The theme that year was Rickshaw Ralley. I went all out for my class of 3-and 4-year old's. We had a pretend koi pond in our room. I wore a kimono style shirt with chopsticks in my hair. This was my first big time teaching, and to say it was life changing was an understatement. One night during snack time, our VBS director (also my mom) came up to my class, and they proudly told her what they had learned that day. "Go fish for Jesus!" "What are we going to fish for?" the other teacher proudly asked. The kids excitedly shouted in

response,"FISH!" Even though I had prepped, I made class fun, I called each child by name... the lesson missed the mark. They didn't really have a clue what the great commission really meant.

We don't want to just entertain children. (No matter how fun things are.)

We don't want to just provide a babysitting service. (Eternity is too important to waste our time.)

We don't want to create a culture where kids can quote scripture and key points but not have the heart change that goes with it.

Our goal as kidmin leaders should be to see boys and girls walking in relationship with Christ, for life. We want to create resilient disciples.

It doesn't matter how amazing your VBS is if kids aren't walking with Christ.

It doesn't matter how much money you raised for missions if kids aren't walking with Christ.

It doesn't matter how many verses they memorize or how many friends they bring if they aren't walking with Christ.

That's the goal. Discipleship. Seeing children walking with Jesus. [period]

What does resilient discipleship look like though, and how do we get there? Well, unfortunately this chapter isn't going to have all the answers. There is not a 5-point outline you can follow for guaranteed success. (But please keep reading, though!)

Resilient discipleship can be defined as a Christ-follower – a person that walks in relationship (intimacy) with Christ. It's a committed relationship with Jesus, and it should last a lifetime.

This is our big goal – to see children walking with Christ for life, growing in their relationship with him. Like with any goal, unless we have a plan in place a goal doesn't go anywhere. Without steps to make a goal into reality, it's just a wish.

Do you have a plan in place that results in children (without prompting from adults in their lives) accepting Christ as their Lord and Savior and walking with him? You need a plan!

You've heard our team talk before about the importance of a curriculum roadmap. (Curriculum is a tool you can use to get you where you want to go.) You've read magazine articles or have watched training videos where we talk about being intentional in your ministry in everything from the games you play to the way you lead worship. What you do matters… for so many reasons.

What if there is no plan? What if you are just providing a safe place for boys and girls to come and have fun while the grown-ups are in church? Those children might not know Jesus personally, intimately. They might not stand on the authority of God's Word, trusting it as their guide through life. Because there was no intentionality in church, they may turn away. Eternal decisions could be made.

So how are resilient disciples made, then?

Show kids Jesus. [period]

Teach them his Word. Invite boys and girls to walk with and follow him. Let them experience his radical love. Model discipleship. Equip mom and dad. Walk beside families.

In John 8:31-32, Jesus is explaining what a disciple looks like. He says "if you hold to my teaching." Other translations say, "if you continue in my Word." We most definitely need to be giving the Gospel to boys and girls every single time. We need to tell boys and girls about the problem with sin and just how much Jesus loves them. Resilient disciples have been changed by the Gospel, but it doesn't stop there. Like Jesus tells in John chapter 8, they need to continue in his Word.

How important is the Word of God in your ministry?

How important is the Word of God in your life as both a Christ follower and a kidmin leader?

If kids continue in his Word….

It's our job, kidmin leaders, to teach children about Jesus, to show them how to walk with him, to teach them his story, and to help them to grow. Discipleship isn't only on Sunday, though. While you (and your team) are responsible for Sunday morning programing, a resilient disciple has fruit on all of the other days of the week too.

Teach kids how to be Jesus followers Sunday to Sunday and every day in between. Show children what it means to be a Jesus follower for life. Model it. Teach it. Shout it from the roof tops. Go crazy at VBS and never pass up an opportunity to have a silly string fight, for sure. Decorate big. Make the Bible come alive in creative and sometimes messy ways. But above all, always remember why you do what you do. We want to see kids walking with Jesus, to be growing in their relationship with him, for life. It's all about Jesus. [period]

| LIVING IT OUT |

- *Is your ministry seeing children become resilient disciples?*

- *How can you help families stay resilient?*

- *Think through your curriculum, programming, worship, and even family resources. Is it all helping to intentionally grow disciples and keep kids in the Word?*

MEET YOUR AUTHORS

BETH FRANK loves Jesus, her hubs, her three girls, and thinking creatively. Beth is the co-founder of KidzMatter. She also owns a design company called B Frank Design Co. She was inspired by her oldest daughter's autism diagnosis to write the book "Ausomely Blessed."

RYAN FRANK is a pastor, publisher, and entrepreneur. He serves as CEO of KidzMatter, co-founder of KidzMatter Mega-Con, and CEO of Frank Insurance Agency. Ryan and his wife, Beth, run several businesses and love to travel and spend time with their three daughters. ryanfrank.com

HANNAH BOLVI lives in the mountains of North Carolina with her wonderful husband, Ethan, and their two adorable daughters, nine-year-old Lily and four-year-old Violet. She is currently serving in her 8th year with Operation Christmas Child. Prior to joining Samaritan's Purse, Hannah worked as a Children's Ministry Director at a large church in Ohio, where she served kids and students of all ages.

AMBER PIKE is the editor of *KidzMatter Magazine*, an author, children's minister, and momma whose passion is to see kids loving the Word of God and walking with Him! Amber is the author of "Exploring the Bible Through History," "The Family Cookbook Devotional," and "Top 50 Ordinary People in God's Extraordinary Plan." Amberpike.org

NATALIE ABBOTT spends her days herding her 5 kids, stealing time with her husband, and teaching people about Jesus. She's the co-founder and Chief Content Officer of Dwell Differently, a company that helps people memorize and meditate on God's Word.

JOSH ZELLO is Hannah's husband and Avery's dad. He serves as family ministry director at Redemption City Church in Baltimore, MD. You can find him drinking coffee, reading books, and wearing funny socks, or at preschoolpastor.com.

JASON HOUSER founded the Seeds Family Worship ministry 18 years ago and has led teams in creating over 200 scripture worship songs and videos to help kids and parents sing God's Word. He has co-written well known CCM songs "Broken Things" and "The Motions" and also co-wrote a parenting discipleship book called Dedicated with Bobby and Chad Harrington.

BRIAN DEMBOWCZYK is the author of Cornerstones: 200 Question and Answers to Learn Truth, Cornerstones: 200 Questions and Answers to Teach Truth, and Gospel-Centered Kids Ministry. Brian served in church ministry for 17 years and was the Managing Editor of The Gospel Project. He holds a Ph.D. from Midwestern Baptist Theological Seminary.

VALERIE BELL is an author and public speaker who communicates her faith with gentle humor and honesty. She has written numerous books, her latest being "RESILIENT: Child Discipleship and the Fearless Future of the Church" (2020). Valerie currently serves as CEO Emerita of Awana Clubs International.

ESTHER MORENO, a nationally recognized voice in Children's Ministry, is an author, speaker, and influencer with a contagious passion for training others to effectively capture the hearts and minds of children with the Gospel of Jesus Christ. Together with her husband, GUYLANDO MORENO, Esther founded Child's Heart Ministries,

LLC, (www.childsheart83.com), which is dedicated to helping churches, parents, and children's ministry workers to move beyond the status quo and make the necessary investments required to become the church that this generation so desperately needs.

RAISEUP FAITH (www.raiseupfaith.com) is a curriculum platform that brings Bible-based lessons and digital resources from a range of trusted kids' ministries, to help see kids grow up to live inspiring lives rooted in Jesus.

ABBY KOONTZ and her husband Jay live in Indiana with their two children, and they are all blessed to be a licensed foster family. Abby is a Licensed Clinical Social Worker. She has worked with children and families involved with the Department of Child Services and Juvenile probation for 14 years. Abby loves her local church and serves in a variety of ministries there including with children and teens.

CINDY BULTEMA loves the Lord, loves life, loves her family, and loves to celebrate! Cindy has over 20 years of ministry experience including currently serving as the Executive Director of GEMS Girls' Clubs. She's a sought-after women's speaker and author of two best-selling Bible studies, Red Hot Faith and Live Full, Walk Free. Connect with Cindy at www.cindybultema.com.

COURTNEY WEAVER works at David C Cook as the marketing manager for curriculum resources—including Wonder Ink—and as the lead strategist for MinistrySpark.com. With a degree in public relations, and a minor in biblical studies, she serves in her local church as the worship leader. She has two sons with her husband, Andrew, and believes engaging kids in God's Word and worship is for more than Sundays. Learn more about Wonder Ink at WonderInk.org today.

STEPHEN "DOC" HUNSLEY, M.D. is the Executive Director and founder of SOAR Special Needs in Lenexa, Kansas. SOAR (Special Opportunities, Abilities, and Relationships) serves over 1000 individuals with disabilities through regular respite events and Special Needs Day Camps. Doc is currently assisting over 500 churches locally, nationally, and globally in starting a Disability Ministry. Doc also organizes the Wonderfully Made Conference held annually every October in Kansas City. Doc is a retired pediatrician while his wife, Kay, continues practicing pediatrics. They are proud parents to three beautiful children: Luke, Mark, and Sarah. The Hunsley's middle child, Mark, is presently running the halls of heaven. During Mark's five-year earthly stay, he gave his family the opportunity to learn from and love a child with autism. You can follow SOAR on Facebook or Connect with Doc on Twitter: @DocHunsley SOARSpecialNeeds.org.

DEBBIE RHOADS has been in ministry for over 30 years, with over 20 of those years being in Children's Ministry. Her ministry roles have included Next Gen Executive Pastor and Leadership Development Director. Debbie lives with her husband, Rob in Franklin, Tennessee where she is the Children's Ministry Director at Grace Chapel. In between her ministry and studies at Liberty University to complete her Psychology: Christian Counseling degrees, she enjoys traveling and being "Gigi" to her two adorable grandchildren.

CPSIA information can be obtained
at www.ICGtesting.com
Printed in the USA
BVHW032242280922
648281BV00005B/20

9 781088 061565